FEB 19

PUBLIC PROFILES

Royal Couples

HARRY AND MEGHAN MARKLE, WILLIAM AND KATE MIDDLETON,
AND CHARLES AND DIANA

The New York Times

PUBLIC PROFILES

Royal Couples

HARRY AND MEGHAN MARKLE, WILLIAM AND KATE MIDDLETON,
AND CHARLES AND DIANA

THE NEW YORK TIMES EDITORIAL STAFF

Published in 2019 by New York Times Educational Publishing in association with The Rosen Publishing Group, Inc.
29 East 21st Street, New York, NY 10010

First Edition

The New York Times
Alex Ward: Editorial Director, Book Development
Brenda Hutchings: Senior Photo Editor/Art Buyer
Phyllis Collazo: Photo Rights/Permissions Editor
Heidi Giovine: Administrative Manager

Rosen Publishing
Greg Tucker: Creative Director
Brian Garvey: Art Director
Megan Kellerman: Managing Editor
Danielle Weiner: Editor

Cataloging-in-Publication Data
Names: New York Times Company.
Title: Royal couples: Harry and Meghan Markle, William and Kate Middleton, and Charles and Diana / edited by the New York Times editorial staff.
Description: New York : The New York Times Educational Publishing, 2019.
| Series: Public profiles | Includes glossary and index.
Identifiers: ISBN 9781642820348 (pbk.) | ISBN 9781642820331 (library bound) | ISBN 9781642820324 (ebook)
Subjects: LCSH: Royal couples—Great Britain—Juvenile literature. | Marriages of royalty and nobility—Great Britain—Juvenile literature. | Harry, Prince, Duke of Sussex, 1984—Juvenile literature. | Meghan, Duchess of Sussex, 1981—Juvenile literature. | William, Prince, Duke of Cambridge, 1982—Juvenile literature. | Catherine, Duchess of Cambridge, 1982—Juvenile literature. | Charles, Prince of Wales, 1948—Juvenile literature. | Diana, Princess of Wales, 1961-1997—Juvenile literature.
Classification: LCC DA591.A45 R693 2019 | DDC 941.086'120922—dc23

Manufactured in the United States of America

On the cover: The Imperial State Crown being carried from the Houses of Parliament in 2016 in London; Dan Kitwood/Getty Images.

Contents

CHAPTER 4

Much Ado About Royals

Introduction

THE BRITISH MONARCHY is often said to be an institution that provides stability and continuity in the United Kingdom.

The reality is more complex. As the monarchy has not had legislative power since 1689, much of thc monarchy's power lies in what the monarchy represents. The royals derive their significance both from their role in continuing the tradition of monarchy and by the ways in which they revolutionize and reconcile that tradition with a modern nation.

The relationships of three particular royal couples — Prince Charles and Lady Diana, Prince William and Duchess Kate, Prince Harry and Meghan Markle — reflect changing social norms throughout the United Kingdom. Lady Diana was born to a family that socialized with royals, and upon her marriage to Prince Charles in 1981, many accepted her as a fitting example of what a princess and future Queen should be. Much has changed in the years since. Lady Diana was mercilessly hounded by the media and suffered from depression and bulimia. Her death in 1997 was attributed in part to the relentless paparazzi who chased her vehicle and may have played a role in the automobile accident that killed her. Diana's struggle throughout her marriage, as well as Prince Charles's known affair with his mistress, Camilla Parker Bowles, softened public opinion on what a royal marriage should, or could, look like. This development is apparent in the relationships that followed.

Duchess Kate, short for Catherine, was born to working-class parents who amassed their own wealth through an online business. She has no royal relation, and when her husband, Prince William, takes the throne, she will be the first Queen of England to have a college education and degree.

Prince Harry, Duke of Sussex, and his wife Meghan, Duchess of Sussex, leave from the West Door of St. George's Chapel, Windsor Castle, on May 19, 2018, in Windsor, England.

Although Prince Harry is sixth in line to the throne, and will likely never be king, his engagement to American actress Meghan Markle has sparked a great deal of international interest. Not only is Meghan an American citizen, she is half African-American, and has had a previous marriage. The royal family would not have embraced these qualities in a potential family member in years prior.

The developments in the royal family tree undoubtedly captivate and influence the public. While the royals may do their best to keep their personal lives private, their relationships are humanizing. They provide a window of public access, brief and curated as it may be. Royal weddings allow the public to interact with and be a part of history. The extensive media coverage prior to and during the royal weddings prompts both the media and the audience to confront why the royal family is so captivating. Reporters often hail royal weddings as welcome respites from the economic or political troubles of the U.K.

Moreover, royal weddings create an opportunity for vendors to capitalize on the surrounding national and international sensationalism. As long as the monarchy keeps up with a changing social culture, it is safe to say that the royal weddings will continue to draw international attention.

CHAPTER 1

Prince Charles and Diana Spencer

The royal wedding of Prince Charles and Lady Diana represented a fable-like, picturesque monarchy. Despite the emblematic nature of their marriage and the widespread adoration of Diana, the marriage was troubled. Prince Charles had a mistress, Camilla Parker Bowles, and Diana struggled with depression and an eating disorder. The public fascination of Diana continued through her divorce. The dissolution of the marriage, the decline of Diana's mental health, and her tragic death in an automobile accident ultimately turned the media's lens on itself and on Britain.

Royal Romance and Princely Duty

BY WILLIAM BORDERS | MARCH 22, 1981

"NOW THAT HE'S GETTING A WIFE, isn't it time he had a proper job as well?"

While blunt, this statement by a London radio announcer pinpointed the problem behind the happy news of Prince Charles's engagement last month to Lady Diana Frances Spencer, an endearingly shy and lovely 19-year-old aristocrat.

The question of what Prince Charles should do with the ablest years of his life as he waits in the wings to succeed his mother troubles many people, not least of them, Queen Elizabeth. It would be nice, the Queen once said as she pondered the matter with a group of her most trusted advisers, if there were some way Charles could avoid what she called "the Edward VII situation."

By the time Edward VII became King, upon the death of his mother, Queen Victoria, he was an ill-prepared 59-year-old grandfather, best known for decades of idleness and debauchery in the parlors and bedrooms of the upper classes. Charles, who is now 32, seems a much more conscientious heir-apparent than Edward, his great-great-grandfather. But, as Charles's mother, who is 54 years old, shows no signs of intending to abdicate, he, too, is likely to be into his 50's, if not older, by the time he ascends to the throne.

Unlike Victoria, who precipitated "the Edward VII situation" by isolating her heir from anything of significance, Queen Elizabeth has carefully introduced her son to many of the burdens of the office he will one day inherit and has kept him abreast of all important developments. Charles has regular access (which his father, Prince Phillip, does not) to the hand-tooled leather boxes of secret Cabinet papers that daily stream across the sovereign's desk, and he often discusses matters of state with Government leaders. When the Queen is abroad, he, as senior councilor of State, is empowered to act in her place. He can conduct a meeting of the privy council, a kind of supercabinet of political elders, and he can give the royal assent to bills. Still, it doesn't amount to all that much. From time to time, it has been suggested that Charles serve in some official capacity in Australia, or that he become a kind of roving ambassador, spending extended periods of time in various parts of the British Commonwealth, but neither of these proposals seems to be under serious consideration at present.

For now, however, the royal family's attention, and that of much of the world, is centered on the impending marriage. The wedding of Charles and Diana in St. Paul's Cathedral on July 29 is likely to be one of the most glittering royal occasions of the century. It will give the hard-pressed British people an emotional lift and at least momentarily divert their attention from the country's serious economic problems. Certainly their attention was diverted by the appearance at a benefit concert of the young Lady Diana in a strapless black gown that evoked "audible admiring gasps," reported a breathless BBC announcer.

The young lovers have become the objects of something approaching adoration. Doubtless this will be demonstrated when Prince Charles soon makes two trips to the United States, which he has said he always enjoys visiting because he gets along so well with Americans, and they with him. His first visit begins on April 30 with a tour of the naval base at Norfolk, Va. and ends with a White House dinner on May 1. Then, on June 17, in his capacity as president of the Friends of Covent Garden, Charles will make his first overnight visit to New York City. The occasion will be a gala performance of "Sleeping Beauty" by the Royal Ballet of Covent Garden, which this year celebrates its 50th anniversary. To the obvious question, Buckingham Palace says, no, it has not yet been decided whether he will take his fiancee. But New Yorkers are hopeful.

Americans have always have had a fondness for monarchies — they just don't want to live under one. For the British, however, the long-awaited marriage is also substantively important to Britain in constitutional and social terms. For the monarchy "has been one of the few success stories in British 20th-century history," as Lord Blake, a constitutional historian, put it the other day. "Amid economic and political decline, the dissolution of the Empire, and the exhausting struggles of two terrible wars, it has stood out as a monument to stability." To be sure, there are many Britons who find the trappings of monarchy a bit silly. But the institution itself, with all its foibles, remains almost immune to criticism. In fact, its popularity has actually increased over the years as (and partly because) the political power of the monarch has diminished. Of his own interim position, Charles admits that "a Prince of Wales has to do what he can by influence, not power. There isn't any power. The influence is in direct ratio to the respect people have for you." In his case, that respect seems to be substantial, and growing.

And it did not escape notice that on the very same morning the royal engagement was announced in London, a king not much older than Charles was saving the fragile new democracy in Spain by using his personal prestige and the strength of his monarchy to quash a military coup.

The last serious threat to the British monarchy was the crisis of 1936, when Queen Elizabeth's uncle tried to make a divorced woman, Wallis Simpson, his Queen. When the Government objected to the alliance, Edward VIII (later the Duke of Windsor) abdicated, giving as his reason that he could not "discharge my duties as King as I would wish to do without the help and support of the woman I love." According to friends of the royal family, the memory of that abdication, which rocked the very foundation of the monarchy, still haunts Buckingham Palace. It has, in fact, been fresher in recent years because, although no one much liked to say so, Prince Charles's long bachelorhood reminded people of that previous Prince of Wales, also a vigorous and popular young man who traveled the world with great style and charm and had a special rapport with his subjects. That reminder is one reason why a surge of relief followed the announcement that Charles is not only finally getting married, but marrying someone so eminently suited to be the future Queen and helpmeet of Britain's next sovereign. Though not of royal birth, Lady Diana, the youngest daughter of the 8th Earl Spencer, is decidedly top drawer. She and Prince Charles are seventh cousins once removed and her family tree is heavy with titles. The Spencers have been related and close to royalty for centuries.

When Lady Diana's parents were married in 1954, the Queen and Prince Philip were among the guests. Lady Diana's father, who suffered a slight stroke a few years ago, had been equerry (personal attendant) to both King George VI and the present Queen, who is godmother to the Earl's son, Lady Diana's brother, Charles. And Lady Diana's maternal grandmother, Ruth, Lady Fermoy, is an intimate friend of the Queen Mother's.

The divorce of Diana's parents, when she was only 7 years old, was the major event of her childhood, she has told friends. And, they say, it strengthened her determination to have a happy marriage herself. (In divorce proceedings, each of Diana's parents was publicly identified as a "guilty party," which would have made them distinctly unwelcome at court just a few years ago. But, presumably, Princess Margaret's divorce from Lord Snowdon in 1978 has made it more difficult to point the royal finger in admonition.)

After her parents' divorce, Lady Diana lived with her father, who won custody of her, her brother and her sisters Sarah and Jane. Her mother, whom Diana resembles, quickly married Peter Shand Kydd, a wallpaper heir with whom she now lives on a remote estate in Scotland. For a while, Diana and her mother were estranged, but they were reconciled several years ago and have since become much closer. Lord Spencer, an avid amateur photographer who enjoys conducting tourists around his house, lives in one of the grandest in all England with his second wife, Raine, the daughter of romantic novelist Barbara Cartland.

When the new bride and groom, both of whom love the country, move into Highgrove, the nine-bedroom Georgian house in the Cotswolds that Charles bought last year for about $2 million, it will be a distinct step down from the splendor of Lady Diana's family seat. Althorp, an enormous 16th-century mansion in Northamptonshire, contains one of the finest private art collections in all of England, including portraits by Van Dyck, Reynolds and Gainsborough.

Lady Diana's childhood was spent at her father's other country home, in Sandringham, Norfolk, very close to the royal residence there, and she and her two older sisters and her younger brother were frequent playmates and birthday party guests of the young royals. Ever since, there have been many contacts with the royal family.

But Charles and Diana's first real meeting, they now recall, occurred in 1977, when he was a guest at a shooting weekend on her father's Northamptonshire estate. The relationship became serious only last July when Diana went to Balmoral, the royal estate in Scotland, to visit her sister, Lady Jane Fellowes, whose husband is assistant private secretary to the Queen.

After a low-profile courtship conducted mostly at the country homes of friends and family, Charles finally proposed early in February, during a private dinner in his Buckingham Palace apartment, an elegant but comfortably cluttered three-room suite on the south side of the building, which is separated by 150 yards of corridor from his parents' quarters. Lady Diana was about to leave on a vacation in Australia with her mother and stepfather. "I wanted to give her a chance to think about it — to think if it was all going to be too awful," the Prince explained, but Diana has since said she "never had any doubts." During the February vacation, on a secluded beach in New South Wales, mother and daughter "of course talked about Diana's future life," Mrs. Shand Kydd now says. "I'm sure she can cope, and learn quickly."

One thing Diana has already learned is to wear flat-heeled shoes. She is tall — only about an inch shorter than Charles — and has made a point of not wearing high heels since she started going out with him. The photographs of them on their engagement day were taken on the steps of Buckingham Palace with her, perhaps at the photographer's suggestion, standing one step below him, thereby creating the illusion that he is several inches taller. To the delight of her future subjects, the royal bride-to-be is no idle, languid debutante given to hanging around nightclubs but, rather, a hard-working kindergarten teacher who blushes engagingly whenever she encounters press photographers.

Lady Diana is also — it begins to sound like a fable, which may be why it is so enchanting — genuinely beautiful, with strawberry blond hair, blue-gray eyes, and a shy elfin smile that can be dazzling at times. She is also possessed of a keen sense of rectitude and fair play. Thus, although she was prepared to endure the pre-engagement press scrutiny in good humor "because they are only doing their job," she was truly appalled when one newspaper carried a completely fictional account of a "tryst" she and Charles allegedly had late one night on the royal train.

"She's really a sweet and kind person who just loves children," says one of the three girls with whom Lady Diana lived in the $250,000 South Kensington apartment Lord Spencer bought for his daughter

Lady Diana Spencer, the future Diana, Princess of Wales, at a polo match in Hampshire, 1981.

when she moved to London after attending the socially exclusive West Heath Boarding School for Girls in Kent and a finishing school in Switzerland. At the kindergarten where she taught, Lady Diana, whom the children called "Miss Diana," is universally praised as "warm hearted," "gentle," "patient with children" and "low key." One of her co-workers has said that "she made it very easy to forget that her father was rich, and an earl."

In a consideration that was very important to Prince Charles, the future Queen of England is not known "to have been seriously involved with other men," as The Times of London so primly put it. Indeed, in an age of loose morals, that standard may have been one reason for selecting someone so young. Lady Diana has what one Englishman called "a history but no past." By contrast, it is widely thought that Prince Charles has plenty of both. Although the British press has listed more than 20 women with whom the Prince allegedly has been romantically involved over the last 10 or so years, only a handful were ever serious matrimonial contenders: Lady Jane Wellesley, daughter of the 8th Duke of Wellington, is generally thought to have voluntarily pulled out of the race, unwilling to endure the exposure. Davina Sheffield, who was very near the top of the list five years ago, was abrupty dropped after a former beau declared that she would, indeed, make a fine wife for the Prince, and that he ought to know because he had lived with her for a while himself in a thatched cottage. The only royal princess on the list was Marie-Astrid of Luxembourg, but though Charles's mother is known to have thought well of her, as a Roman Catholic, Marie-Astrid could not by British law become queen. Diana's older sister, Lady Sarah Spencer, removed herself from the running when she publicly declared that she was not interested in marrying the Prince. Now that Charles has made his choice — and Diana her's — their principal duty after marriage will be to settle down and produce heirs to keep the line of the House of Windsor going. The newlyweds' country home will be more than comfortably furnished. Looking after it and them will be a staff of half a dozen or more servants, including Prince Charles's two valets, who look after his extensive wardrobe, which includes an array of military uniforms and ceremonial robes.

The young couple will also acquire a residence in London. Clarence House, where Charles lived before his mother ascended to the throne, is the obvious choice, but it is now the home of Queen Elizabeth the Queen Mother, and no one has been presumptuous enough to suggest that she move. It is more likely, therefore, that the young couple will settle in some place like Kensington Palace, where Princess Margaret and other royals live.

There is, however, no question of Charles and Diana's being able to maintain however many residences they may acquire. Although the Prince of Wales is not on the civil list — the Government pay-roll for royals — his extensive hereditary land holdings make him, already, one of the richest members of his family. Through holdings of the Duchy of Cornwall, Charles owns more than 100,000 acres scattered around the country, some of them in London, which bring him an income of about $500,000 a year. At age 21, he voluntarily arranged to turn over half of that income to the Government, in lieu of taxes. (The royal family do not pay income or inheritance taxes, which is the key to their enormous wealth.) The understanding at the time was that some part of the monies might revert to him on his marriage. And when he becomes King, Charles will come into the immensely greater fortune — perhaps as high as $140 million — that is now the Queen's, as monarch. "My father was frightened of his mother; I was frightened of my father, and I am damned well going to see to it that my children are frightened of me," was how King George V, who was the father of both Edward VIII and George VI, Queen Elizabeth's father, once put it. And so they were.

By contrast, Charles has a close and happy relationship with his parents. According to those close to him, he tried hard in his childhood to emulate his father. But it was difficult. Prince Philip has always been debonair and almost rakishly handsome; Charles, though now possessed of an easy public manner, has always been personally somewhat shy and extremely self-conscious about such physical imperfections as his jug ears. Father and son do, however, have moments of great intimacy enjoying such country pasttimes as shooting and fishing, as well as a more boisterous relationship in such sports as polo.

As he has matured, however, Charles has moved much closer to his mother, and the two of them have an extremely warm relationship that finds no parallel elsewhere in the family. "It's natural when you stop and think about it," says a family friend. "The two of them share a special fate, a role in history that excludes all the others."

Besides his parents, Charles was most influenced by the late Earl Mountbatten of Burma, his father's uncle and a national hero. Mountbatten was the grandfather Charles had never really known. With him he could discuss many things, including his love life, that he couldn't discuss with his parents. When Mountbatten was killed by Irish republican terrorists in 1979, Charles was shattered. The affection and admiration were mutual. Before Mountbatten's death, when someone suggested to him that Britain was lucky in having this particular heir to the throne, Mountbatten replied, "It's not luck at all. It's a bloody miracle." As for the rest of the family, Charles is so much older than his brothers, Andrew, 21, and Edward, 17, that his relationship to them is almost more paternal than fraternal. Since their personalities are so different, Charles is not particularly close to his sister, Anne, 30, who has a reputation for surliness, and he has little in common with her husband, Mark Phillips, a former army officer.

But he is very close to his grandmother, the Queen Mother, who is said to see in Charles the gentleness and strength of character that made her husband, King George VI, such an effective leader during World War II. It is significant that when Lady Diana moved into the protective cocoon of the royal family on the very day her engagement was announced, it was in the Queen Mother's London home that she took up residence. The only one of the inner family circle not born to royalty, the Queen Mother is expected to play a key role in initiating Lady Diana into its mysteries. It is not overstating the case to say that this appealing young woman, who will be known as Her Royal Highness, the Princess of Wales, will help to determine the future of the British monarchy, an ancient institution that depends enormously on the personalities and public images of its leading players. Just as the institution can be damaged by bad behavior — witness Edward VIII's abdication and Victoria's prolonged period of reclusiveness following her husband's death — it can be greatly enhanced by what is publicly perceived as proper behavior on the part of the royal family.

Not only are dignity and probity essential, but so is a certain aloofness, a quality that it will be Diana's task, as much as Charles's, to preserve. Anthony Sampson, the British journalist and social critic, takes this view of the mystical formula that, long after the sun has set on the Empire, somehow still makes Britain the Rolls-Royce of monarchies:

"Between this fairyland palace and the practical world, there is … a drawbridge, which is only let down on special occasions.… There is not so much secrecy that the public eventually loses interest, but there is enough hidden to stimulate intense public curiosity."

To Charles, court protocol is instinctive. Before he was 3 years old, he had learned to bow before getting a kiss from "Gan Gan," Queen Mary, and not to sit down in the presence of his grandfather, King George, until asked to do so.

Despite his jokey mateyness, despite his willingness to put onto his head anything any native anywhere offers him, Charles has well learned the lesson of aloofness. He will not tolerate even the slightest deviation from strict royal protocol. Since he became an adult, he has insisted on being called "Sir," even by girls he was dating.

Charles has only a very few close friends, almost all of them from the moneyed upper class whose weekend pleasures center on huge country estates, where Charles can be himself. Among the inner circle are Nicholas Soames, grandson of Winston Churchill, and Lord and Lady Tryon, who are his hosts every August for a couple of weeks at their lodge in a remote corner of Iceland, where he fishes and catches up on his reading. It adds up to a rather one-dimensional social life, and it seems too bad that the future king cannot relax with other people in his realm. On the other hand, as long as his is everybody's favorite name to drop — and it always will be — it is difficult for him to branch out and still retain the covenant of secrecy by which his real friends protect him. "You learn through experience how to sense who are the ones that are sucking up and who are being genuine," the Prince once said candidly. "But, of course, the trouble is that very often the worst people come up first and the really nice people hang back."

It is impossible to exaggerate the electricity sparked by the mere presence of Charles in a room. Grown men — captains of industry, brilliant artists, ruthless politicians — become as giggly and nervous as excited children as they queue up to bow before him and invariably forget afterward just what was said. Charles recognizes this as an obstacle to any kind of real communication: "One finds you meet people and you have to get through a certain amount of anxiety, or nervousness, or prejudice or whatever, to start with, and it usually takes about 20 minutes or so (before) people are beginning to relax ... and then you've got to go."

This is another aspect of what Sampson calls "the psychological moat," and it is a measure of how effectively Queen Elizabeth has preserved this that it is laughably inconceivable that she should never be seen riding a bicycle in public, as do some of the Scandinavian monarchs. The British royals never try to act like common people, and there is no sign that the British people want them to. "If you begin to poke about it, you cannot reverence it," Walter Bagehot, the 19th-century constitutional analyst, wrote of the monarchy. "Its mystery is its life. We must not let in daylight upon magic."

The desire to preserve the mystical aura around the monarch also helps to explain why Queen Elizabeth's abdication, the most obvious solution to the "Edward VII situation" facing Charles, seems unlikely. "Kingship is not a job, but a status," The Times of London declared recently, urging an end to all talk of abdication. Another argument against abdication is that, except for the disgraceful memory of 1936, there is no tradition of abdication in Britain and, in monarchy, tradition is all. Moreover, there is a genuine governmental value in the continuity that a monarch of long standing can bring to the affairs of state. Although Queen Elizabeth is only 54 years old, she has already practiced her close constitutional relationship with eight prime ministers, stretching back to Winston Churchill. This experience cannot help but add a useful perspective to the regular Tuesday-night meetings on matters of state that she has with Prime Minister Margaret Thatcher—whom she is thought to admire, though any public comment to this effect would be considered highly inappropriate. Prince Charles is often greatly irritated by suggestions that his whole life's work is waiting. "I work bloody hard right now and will continue to," he said not long ago. One essential part of his job is traveling abroad, which he does frequently, as a kind of supersalesman for Britain, which he does well.

He is also kept busy by his many charitable interests and the Prince's Trust, a little-publicized foundation that he specifically designed to assist deprived and disadvantaged youths, especially those from ethnic minorities. Charles often goes out of his way to visit its projects, such as tree-plantings and in-shore rescue squads, and has personally intervened on the part of some of the troubled youths, including one on probation whom he steered to a group of teenagers involved in building dinghies.

More recently, the Prince has been following a program "to find out all I can about every aspect of British life" by spending a complete day learning about the inner workings of Downing Street or the operations of a labor-union office. It is bad form for people to give first-hand impressions on the record, but one Government official who spent the day in a ministry with Charles did note that "he is amazingly bright. He didn't know much detail of what we did, but he seemed to understand all the reasons behind it. I kept thinking that I was in the presence of a natural leader."

Although he is forbidden to discuss politics, Prince Charles's public statements on a variety of subjects are increasingly substantive and even controversial — as, for example, when he irritated businessmen by saying in a speech that "much of British management doesn't seem to understand the importance of the human factor" in labor relations.

The Prince is learning, as he adopts a public personality of his own, that his every word is analyzed. "I can tell you that writing speeches is a major sweat," he says, "worrying whether you're going to say the right thing, because everyone will jump on you." He invariably consults with his parents before delivering his speeches, which he writes himself, but on at least one occasion they chewed him out for overstepping the bounds of propriety in an address he had neglected to clear with them. His private secretary, Edward Adeane, is another adviser and backstopper.

Like his father, and unlike his mother, Charles displays a quick wit in public, even about the monarchy, which he once called "the oldest profession in the world." In a family not noted for its intellectual achievements, he also shows signs of having a good mind. He seldom reads novels, but Aleksandr Solzhenitsyn and E.F. Schumacher, author of "Small Is Beautiful: Economics as if People Mattered," are favorite writers. He loves classical music and plays the cello, although less frequently in recent years, and he is not ashamed to admit that there is a certain passage in Berlioz's "L'Enfance du Christ" that "is so moving I'm reduced to tears every time I hear it."

He yearns to be taken seriously, but often he is not. In a speech at Cambridge a couple of years ago, he made a plea for a more "open-minded" approach to religious education and praised the idea of workers communities in which workers were free to criticize their bosses. When the question period came, a student rose to ask, "Sir, how do you account for your amazing success with women?"

The Prince's physical and athletic exploits are much better known than his mental abilities, probably because they provide better pictures. He is good to excellent at a wide range of hairy-chested outdoor activities, including polo, skiing, riding, shooting and wind-surfing. "I like to see if I can challenge myself to do something that is potentially hazardous, just to see if mentally I can accept the challenge and carry it out," he once said when asked about why he insisted on doing things

Prince Charles, an avid outdoorsman, trekking in the foothills of the Himalayas, Nepal, in December 1980.

like parachute jumping. Anthony Holden, author of the most comprehensive biography of Charles, has a different theory: Forced by his circumstances always to be cautious and guarded in what he says, the Prince is never intellectually challenged, and his received attitudes are never questioned. "Thus he courts physical, rather than intellectual, danger," Holden argues. "The price of such thrills and spills is a deep monotony elsewhere in his life." And now, as this most unusual young man does a perfectly ordinary thing and decides to marry a pretty young woman, Britain's monarchy machine is gearing up for an extravaganza without parallel in any other land. Already, souvenirs are on sale all over the United Kingdom. And Lloyd's of London has issued insurance policies upward of $22 million to cover business losses resulting from a cancellation or delay in the wedding.

Between now and the day of the wedding, July 29, there will be a continuing flood of information about every detail of the festivities. And most of us — even those who won't admit it — will lap it all up, hungrily. While the details of Lady Diana's dress will be kept secret until almost the last moment, it has already been announced that it will be designed by David and Elizabeth Emanuel, creators of the off-the-shoulder black dress that caused such a stir at the Covent Garden fund-raiser. "Lady Diana is young, fresh and lovely, and the dress should emphasize that," the Emanuels have said. "We want to make her look like a fairy princess."

Charles will probably wear a naval uniform, as his father did at his wedding. The bridal attendants will, undoubtedly, include members of both families. There will be a glittering procession of carriages from Buckingham Palace, along a route parallel with the Thames, past huge crowds that will begin to gather the day before. In St. Paul's Cathedral, Sir Christopher Wren's architectural masterpiece in the City of London (the financial district), reportedly chosen because it seats 500 more people than Westminster Abbey, trumpets will sound, choirs will sing and the sentimentally inclined, including almost certainly the Queen, will shed tears of joy. The assembled guests will include a generous representation of Europe's remaining royalty, along with heads of friendly nations as well as numerous dignitaries from every aspect of British life. Wedding gifts will pour in from all over the world. An elegant reception will be held, probably at Buckingham Palace so that the newlyweds may appear on the balcony to show themselves to the gathered multitudes. As for the honeymoon, the Prince's parents spent their's in the British Isles, so he and Diana might do likewise, but the site will be kept secret as long as possible. Queen Elizabeth came to the throne at age 25, in 1952, at a time when Britain was still considered a major world power. Now, Charles conceded recently, it is no more than "a really rather minor state," and who knows what sort of Britain he may ultimately reign over in the 21st century, by which time it is expected that he will have suceeded his mother. Until then, he sees his primary job as leadership — "to help push people along to be encouraged; to warn, advise, amuse … and generally being seen to show an interest."

Sometimes, it all looks like a campaign for political office. "I enjoyed your piece last week," the Prince will call out to a familiar Fleet Street journalist, playing up to the reporter's vanity like a canny old pol. And when you see him visiting, say, a copperpipe factory and listening with rapt attention to a nervous and incomprehensible explanation of why the pipes are different sizes, you almost expect to see an aide walking behind him passing out "Vote for Charles" buttons. According to a friend who has discussed it with him, Charles sees the political campaign comparison as apt — as evidently did a milling-machine operator in a factory the Prince visited recently. "I'd vote for him if he were running for king," the man said afterward.

Though Charles does not campaign in any political sense, he is campaigning all the time for the maintenance of the office that he will someday assume. More and more, he is responsible for the preservation of the British monarchy — which, for many reasons, a great many people seem to think is worth preserving.

Now, at last, he will have someone with whom to share that responsibility.

Charles and Lady Diana Rehearse the Wedding

BY R.W. APPLE JR. | JULY 28, 1981

PRINCE CHARLES AND LADY DIANA SPENCER rehearsed their vows tonight in the hush of St. Paul's Cathedral. Lady Diana, whose nerves have been frayed by the intense scrutiny to which she has been subjected in recent weeks, arrived at the cathedral by way of an underground car park. But after an hourlong practice ceremony, she and her fiance emerged hand-in-hand through the west door. She managed a quick smile for the crowd of several thousand people before jumping with Prince Charles into a waiting car.

For the second day running, enthusiastic throngs surged through central London, clogging streets and paralyzing traffic. Nancy Reagan, who is representing the United States at the wedding, found her carefully designed schedule in tatters. She was 30 minutes late for a wreath-laying ceremony at St. Paul's and even later for a lunch with Princess Margaret at the Princess's apartment in Kensington Palace.

St. Paul's, designed 300 years ago by Christopher Wren, was sealed off by the police earlier in the day. Specialists in terrorism and security locked doors and checked every nook and cranny of the great domed church while colleagues rechecked lists of those who will be in buildings overlooking the processional route Wednesday.

POSITIONS ARE STAKED OUT

A few hardy royalists have already staked out positions on The Mall, down which the Household Cavalry, the antique horse-drawn carriages and police escorts will clatter on their way to the cathedral Wednesday morning. The first in place were a housemistress at a private school in the West Country, Averil Harrison, and her 18-year-old daughter, Rosemary. They set up camp at 2:30 P.M. yesterday.

"We are all prepared with plenty of food," said Mrs. Harrison, who also brought along deck chairs and sleeping bags. "When that runs out, we shall take it in turns to buy some. We have come here for the atmosphere. You can see a lot more on television but you miss actually being involved."

Tonight, Lady Diana and Prince Charles danced at Buckingham Palace at a gala ball that followed a dinner for 90 given by Queen Elizabeth II. Then they said farewell until the moment at 11 A.M. Wednesday when they meet before the high altar of St. Paul's in the midst of all the splendor that the thousand-year-old British monarchy can muster.

Most of the 1,400 guests were either members of the extended family of European royalty or close personal and family friends of the bride and bridegroom. Mrs. Reagan, who had earlier attended the opening performance of the Harlem Dance Theater at the Royal Opera House, Covent Garden, was among them.

As part of the security operation, the police opened manholes this afternoon in central London. Officers using dogs searched potential hiding places for explosives, and others probed the insides of scaffolding poles used to support the bleachers along the route.

Sharpshooters will be stationed on roofs to watch for any sign of an attack by Irish republican guerrillas, particularly if Kieran Doherty or Kevin Lynch, who are on hunger strike at the Maze prison outside Belfast, should die before the wedding. Both are reported to be losing strength rapidly.

"We will rely on people in the crowd to tell us if they see anything unusual," said Commander James Sewell, who is in charge of police operations. "There will be a policeman every four steps on the route as well as a soldier with a fixed bayonet every six paces."

More than 3,000 men from Britain's three military services and from Commonwealth armies will take part in the pageantry and the security operation. None will carry live ammunition.

BROTHERS TO BE 'SUPPORTERS'

In addition to the bride and bridegroom, several members of the royal family are to take part in the wedding ceremony, which is scheduled to start at 11 A.M. (6 A.M. New York time). Instead of a best man, Prince Charles will have as "supporters" his two brothers, Prince Andrew and Prince Edward. Prince Andrew, the elder, will have custody of the ring. Lady Sarah Armstrong-Jones, the 17-year-old daughter of Prince Charles's aunt, Princess Margaret, will be one of the bridesmaids. Lord Nicholas Windsor, 11, the younger son of the Duke and Duchess of Kent, will be one of the pages, or groomsmen.

The other page will be Edward van Cutsem, 8, the son of the horse owner Hugh van Cutsem, one of the Prince's closest friends. The other bridesmaids will be India Hicks, 14, daughter of the interior designer David Hicks and granddaughter of the late Earl Mountbatten of Burma, who served Prince Charles as a surrogate grandfather; Catherine Cameron, 6, whose mother, Lady Cecil Cameron, once dated the Prince; Sarah Jane Gaselee, 10, daughter of Nick Gaselee, who trains Prince Charles's racehorse, and Clementine Hambro, 5, whom Lady Diana once taught at the Young England Kindergarten. Miss Hambro is a great-granddaughter of the late Sir Winston Churchill.

Lady Diana will be given in marriage by her father, Earl Spencer.

An Ocean of Union Jacks and Chanting Throngs Along Procession Route

BY WILLIAM BORDERS | JULY 30, 1981

HUNDREDS OF THOUSANDS of joyful Britons, taking a welcome break from the strains of a difficult summer, lined the route of the royal wedding procession today to cheer their Prince and his bride.

In a patriotic festival spirit, they wept and shouted and danced in the streets, waving a sea of small Union Jacks, and saluting this weary old land with chorus after chorus of "Rule Britannia."

"It's a great day to be British," said Geoffrey Tirson, a 72-year-old retired factory worker, his voice breaking as the Prince and Princess of Wales waved to the crowd from the second-floor balcony of Buckingham Palace.

"I was right here standing on this very spot of grass on the night that Prince Charles was born," Mr. Tirson said. "That seems just like yesterday, and now here he is, married. I say, God bless him and her and all of us."

'WE WANT THE QUEEN!'

The traditional appearance on the balcony, which was draped with a gold-fringed scarlet banner, came moments after the young couple and the rest of the royal family returned from the ceremony at St. Paul's Cathedral, passing through the crowds. Thousands of people slept on the sidewalks last night to make sure of getting a good vantage point today.

"We want the Queen!" they chanted after Charles and Diana went back inside, and in response Queen Elizabeth II came out, to thunderous applause. Then there were chants of "We want the Queen Mum!"

Prince Charles and Princess Diana make their appearance on the balcony of Buckingham Palace after their wedding ceremony at St. Paul's Cathedral, London, England, July 29, 1981.

and out came Queen Elizabeth the Queen Mother, who symbolizes more than any of them the beloved status of the monarchy and the sense of national continuity that it represents.

"We have our problems in this country, but we have our strengths, too, and this is certainly one of them," said Brenda Logan, who, like many in the crowd, was wearing a Union Jack over her shoulders. She unrolled her sleeping bag on Fleet Street before noon yesterday, and spent the 24-hour wait playing Scrabble, listening to the radio, chatting with others in the crowd and eating sandwiches.

Why did she go to so much trouble, when she could have stayed home and got a far better view of the spectacle on television? Her answer was echoed by many others: "It's history, isn't it? I want to be a part of it. I can tell my grandchildren I was actually here where Charles and Di were, not just home watching the telly."

SILLINESS AND FUN

Nearly everyone who was not out cheering seemed indeed to be home watching. Outside the center of London, streets were generally deserted.

Along the route, the overnight scene was a carnival of silliness and fun, a street festival in which all the rules about reserve and not talking to strangers seemed to have been repealed.

A number of young people had painted their faces, hair or chests red, white and blue, like the flag. Six Cambridge University students, in dinner jackets, set a formal table on The Mall and enjoyed an elegant candlelit dinner of poached salmon and champagne. Near dawn, with the temperature in the high 60's, dozens of people splashed merrily in the fountains of Trafalgar Square.

In fact, the revelry was at such a pitch that by the time of the wedding, many people, hung over and exhausted, inadvertently slept in the warm morning sunshine of St. James's Park right through the spectacle that they had come to watch.

ALL-DAY PARTIES

In the hotels and other buildings along the two-mile route, including many newspaper offices, law firms and financial institutions, there were dozens of stylish parties that began shortly after dawn today and lasted into the evening. Pubs along the route stayed open extra late, their patrons happily spilling out onto the littered sidewalks.

Despite the cheery mood, security for the wedding procession was unusually tight, though discreetly so, a reminder of the grim reality that lies behind the fairy-tale world that the wedding represented. One of the splendidly liveried footmen on Charles's horse-drawn carriage was in fact a policeman, and so was one of the Queen's. Policemen were posted on the tops of buildings, and every few yards along the procession, surveying the crowd. But as it happened, they made only one arrest along the entire route — for pickpocketing.

Security officials had been apprehensive about the possibility of some kind of disruption from Irish nationalist guerrillas, who killed Earl Mountbatten of Burma, Prince Charles's great-uncle, two years ago, and who are currently conducting a hunger strike at Maze Prison near Belfast.

There were also fears arising from the rioting that broke out in London and other British cities earlier this month. Most of those disorders have subsided, but they broke out again in Liverpool this week, and early this morning a 22-year-old man died there after being struck by a police vehicle, in circumstances that remained unclear. The incident was under investigation. It was the first death in any of the disorders this month.

CROWD ESTIMATED AT 60,000

But those troubles, and the harsh statistics of Britain's severe economic recession, seemed very far away from the celebrators along the procession route, a crowd that Scotland Yard estimated at 600,000. As the opening bars of "God Save the Queen," played by a band in the forecourt of Buckingham Palace, gave the signal that the procession of 11 horse-drawn carriages was beginning, thousands of cardboard periscopes were raised into position, thousands of cameras clicked in a frenzy and thousands of small children were thrust into the air for the historic view of so many "royals" on parade.

Along the procession route, other bands in stationary positions heralded the imminent arrival of the Queen with the national anthem, sending ripples of excitement ahead of the procession. After it passed each point, thousands of transistor radios were switched on, so that listeners could follow the service, and the church music filled the air.

Whispers, Anger and Doubt As Britons Rally to Princess

BY WILLIAM E. SCHMIDT | JUNE 20, 1992

THERE WAS A POLITE RIPPLE of applause as the carriage carrying Queen Elizabeth II and the Prince of Wales curled beside the grandstand at the Royal Ascot on Tuesday. It was the opening day of the summer season, and the men in top hats and morning coats and the women in pastel dresses were there as much to watch the members of the royal family as the race horses.

But it was the second carriage, the one carrying the Princess of Wales, that caused the commotion. As it approached, the applause began to swell, growing louder and louder. Behind the ropes, some people were shouting, and waving hats in the air. "Di!" one man hollered, above the din. "We're with you!"

NO PUBLIC COMMENT

Two weeks after newspapers in London began printing excerpts from a new book depicting the 30-year-old Princess as abjectly depressed and even suicidal over her marriage to the Prince of Wales, Britons remain alternately enthralled and horrified.

Even now, hardly anyone knows whether the stories — that the Princess on five separate occasions tried to commit suicide, that she suffers from bulimia and depression — are true. No member of the royal family, including Charles and Diana, has offered any public comment about the book or the newspaper accounts.

Still, the telling as much as the tale itself have provoked anger and emotion across Britain; at the same time they have brought a bounty of new readers and profits to the newspapers and publishers flogging the yarn. And for some, who say they fear for the future of the monarchy, the book, "Diana: Her True Story," by Andrew Morton, and its published excerpts have raised large and troubling questions.

Even if Diana and Charles avoid a divorce or separation, many people are saying that the monarchy as an institution is listing badly, a casualty of waning public confidence and the reckless disregard with which they say Britain's popular press now pursues the private lives of the royal family.

The book, by a former tabloid reporter, is already into its fifth printing in Britain, only two days after it went on sale in bookshops. Roughly 180,000 copies have been printed, and its British publisher, Michael O'Mara Books, says it cannot keep up with demand. (The book is also available now in the United States, where it is published by Simon & Schuster.)

Mr. Morton this week defended the book from critics who said it was too intrusive and personal, and relied on too many anonymous sources. "Her friends have stood by the premise of the book," said Mr. Morton, noting that none of the people used as anonymous sources had come forward to deny remarks attributed to them, directly or indirectly. "They have stood by the integrity of the book. It is a very sympathetic portrait of a woman who has been deeply misunderstood."

But even for those who don't particularly care one way or the other about the monarchy, the book has had quite another impact: It has inflamed and enlarged the cult of Diana. She is already a larger-than-life character, and the accounts of her troubles have made her more than just a storybook Princess, reshaping her image into that of a woman and mother with problems and anxieties shared by millions.

"She's one of us now," wrote S. J. Taylor, an American woman who is a journalist living in London, in a guest column this week for The Evening Standard in London.

"People have become so engaged in this story, because people want to project their own values and expectations onto the royals," said Harold Brooks-Baker, the publishing director of Burke's Peerage. "Thanks to the tabloid press and books like Morton's, the royal family has been reduced to nearly fictional characters, where the readers fill in the blanks."

In recent days, there have been broad expressions of public sympathy for Princess Diana. Last week, as she toured a hospice for AIDS patients, the Princess broke down in tears after people in the crowd pushed forward to offer support and encouragement.

Among defenders of the establishment, the flood of published revelations about the marriage of the Prince and Princess of Wales has evoked anger. On Sunday, Sir Peregrine Worsthorne, a longtime editor and columnist of The Daily Telegraph, went so far as to suggest that Andrew Neil, the editor of The Sunday Times, and Rupert Murdoch, the paper's owner, deserved a good lashing for publishing the excerpts from Mr. Morton's book.

"In the good old days when men were men and horsewhips were horsewhips, it would not have been the future of the monarchy we would have had cause to worry about so much as the health and safety, not to say skin, of certain editors and proprietors," Sir Peregrine wrote.

At the same time, a growing number of Members of Parliament, in both the Labor and Conservative Parties, are arguing that it is time again to consider legal restrictions on the press, to keep it from violating the privacy of both public and private figures.

A PRESS COMMISSION

"Accurate news reporting is the oxygen of our democratic process," said Clive Soley, a longtime Labor Party representative from Islington in north London. "And judging from what I've seen in the papers on this matter, and others, I'd say the air is getting pretty polluted. We need to start taking steps to clean it up."

Among other things, there is talk about giving legal authority to a standing press commission, which could enforce sanctions against papers that the commission judges to have violated basic standards of "accuracy and impartiality."

Since Britain has no formal guarantees of freedom of speech and press, there are few constraints on the Government's ability to restrict journalists. But it is doubtful whether such measures could ever pass

Parliament; Prime Minister John Major and his Government have refused to join the debate over press restrictions.

As usual, Buckingham Palace has kept a discreet silence, despite the storm swirling around it. It has not been a good year at the Palace. First, there was the separation of the Duke and Duchess of York, Prince Andrew and Sarah Ferguson. Prince Andrew is a younger brother of Prince Charles. Then, Princess Anne, Charles's sister, announced that she was getting a divorce from her husband, Mark Phillips.

Buckingham Palace has generally kept silent; spokesmen beg off calls from reporters with their usual response — no comment. In fact they are even reticent about replying to a reporter's question about whether there is a legal or constitutional restraint that would keep a divorced prince from becoming king. The answer is no, Prince Charles, even if divorced, could become King.

In some way, the emotional response to what is happening to Prince Charles and Princess Diana underscores a curious phenomenon: At the same time people seem more drawn to the latest chapter in the story, they have less and less faith in the monarchy itself.

While the monarchy endures as one of Britain's more favored institutions — scoring well ahead of the church, Parliament and the press in terms of public confidence — there has been an erosion of popular support, according to a survey last week by Market and Opinion Research International, a London polling firm.

Charles and Diana Are Separating 'Amicably'

BY WILLIAM E. SCHMIDT | DEC. 10, 1992

BUCKINGHAM PALACE wrote the unhappy ending today to a storybook marriage gone badly wrong, a seven-sentence-long announcement that Charles, the Prince of Wales and heir to the British throne, and Diana, the Princess of Wales, had agreed to separate after 11 years as husband and wife.

Prime Minister John Major, who broke the news in a nationally televised appearance before a hushed House of Commons, sought to cushion the blow by emphasizing that the royal couple did not intend to divorce and would continue to carry on their royal and constitutional duties separately as the future King and Queen of England.

MONARCHY IN UPHEAVAL

"This decision has been reached amicably and they will both continue to participate fully in the upbringing of their children," Mr. Major said, reading from the text.

But historians and students of the royal family said the separation confronted the monarchy with its most serious upheaval since 1936, when King Edward VIII abdicated in order to marry the divorced American socialite Wallis Simpson.

Among other things, the arrangement poses difficult questions about how, exactly, the monarchy will function in the future, with the Prince and Princess leading separate lives, inside separate palaces, surrounded by separate and potentially rival courts.

BRITONS SEEM STUNNED

It also raises doubts on a more human level: can the ancient protocols and traditions of the monarchy accommodate the tricky conventions of marriage and family in the 1990's, with the special demands of single parenthood and joint custody? Even trickier, will the royal couple be able to date other people?

The sudden announcement seemed to stun many Britons, despite months of intense speculation in British newspapers that the marriage that began in 1981 as a fairy tale come true had devolved into a loveless affair, with the Prince and the Princess living all but separate lives.

When the Prince wed the former Lady Diana Spencer in July 1981, their marriage was breathlessly described as "the wedding of the century," a spectacle of pomp and pageantry broadcast to millions of viewers around the world. The Princess, in particular, went on to become a beloved icon of the British monarchy, widely admired in Britain and beyond for her coolness and style.

Today, even as the announcement was being read in Parliament, Prince Charles, who is 44, and the Princess, 31, were in different parts of Britain. He was visiting an old people's home and addressing a business luncheon north of London; she was visiting a clinic in northeast England. Neither made any remarks referring to the separation.

The gravity of today's announcement was underscored by Mr. Major, who is in the midst of preparing for a critical summit meeting of European leaders in Edinburgh this weekend. He was forced to cancel a scheduled afternoon meeting with Jacques Delors, the president of the European Community, in order to read the palace statement to the House of Commons.

Both Mr. Major and the palace insisted that the line of succession to the throne was unaffected, and the Prime Minister even told Parliament there was nothing in the decision to prevent the Princess of Wales from someday being crowned as Queen Consort.

He said the Prince and Princess only intended to live separately while jointly rearing their two sons, Princes William, 10, and Harry, 8.

At the same time, the Church of England issued a statement saying the Prince, as the future King, could preside as head of the church despite the breakup of his marriage.

There is no modern precedent for a divorced or separated monarch. George IV was the last British King whose marriage broke up; he left his wife, Caroline of Brunswick, in 1796, a year after they were married.

DIVORCE IS PREDICTED

Harold Brooks-Baker, the publishing director of Burke's Peerage, said he believed today's announcement was only the precursor to the couple's eventual divorce, which he said could pose more difficult questions about Prince Charles's ascension to the throne. While there is no constitutional bar to a divorced prince ascending to the throne, Mr. Brooks-Baker said it would complicate matters by effectively barring Prince Charles from remarrying.

"In such a situation, I wouldn't be surprised if Charles might decide to renounce the throne himself, in favor of his elder son, William," he said.

On street corners, in pubs and in the corridors of Parliament tonight, there was heartfelt expressions of sympathy for Queen Elizabeth II, after a year she herself last month described as her "annus horribilis."

The announcement today means that all three marriages of her children have broken down. Andrew, the Prince of York, separated from the Duchess of York this year amid a messy public scandal that involved the publication of photographs of the Duchess cavorting topless beside a swimming pool with another man.

Princess Anne, the Queen's only daughter, divorced Mark Phillips in the summer. She is scheduled to embark on her second marriage this weekend, when she will wed a naval commander at a private ceremony in the north of England. The queen has a fourth child, Edward, who is not married.

QUEEN TO FOOT BILLS

The news of the separation comes at a time when the credibility of the monarchy is at a modern lowpoint as a result of persistent reports alluding to the marital scandals and wealthy life style of some members of the royal family.

Two weeks ago, in what appeared to be a bid to defuse public resentment, the Queen took the extraordinary step of breaking with royal tradition, announcing not only that she would now pay tax on her personal income but that she would also absorb a larger share of the public expenses of some members of the royal family.

The reason for the timing of today's announcement was not clear, since the palace said the matter of the separation had been under discussion privately for some time.

Aides at Downing Street said Mr. Major had been kept informed of discussions within the palace about the royal couple, but was not directly involved in the decision to make a public announcement today. Mr. Major, who last saw the Queen a week ago, was first told about the planned announcement on Tuesday evening, a spokesman said.

NO 'THIRD PARTY,' PALACE SAYS

In background remarks to reporters, the palace also took pains tonight to emphasize that what they called a "third party" was not involved in the couple's decision to separate.

In recent months, unconfirmed press reports in Britain have suggested that both the Prince and Princess might have had other romantic interests. Prince Charles was said to be closer to Camilla Parker Bowles, an old girlfriend, than to his wife; the Princess, according to a reported transcript of an intercepted mobile telephone conversation, had had a long and intimate conversation with an unnamed man who called her "Squidgy" and said he loved her.

There have been recurrent reports over the years that the Prince and Princess were growing apart, their differences magnified over time. He likes solitary days on the moors, hunting and fishing; she prefers family beach outings. He is fond of classical music; she adores pop. He immerses himself in books about history and architecture and organic gardening; she reads light romantic novels.

At the same time, the Princess emerged more and more as a person in her own right, plunging into charity causes and speaking out on AIDS.

But the first hint of deeper marital difficulties followed the publication this summer of a book that purported to describe the terrible personal toll the marriage had taken on the Princess. "Diana: Her True Story," written by Andrew Morton, a former newspaper reporter who covered Buckingham Palace, not only said the Princess felt "trapped in a loveless marriage," but suffered from bulimia and had tried to commit suicide on at least five occasions.

Mr. Morton said he based his reporting on friends of the Princess, and she herself never disavowed any of its details. Instead, by showing herself in public with some of the people Mr. Morton quoted, there were suggestions she was in fact endorsing their remarks.

More recently, Mr. Morton disclosed that Prince Philip, the Queen's husband, had written his daughter-in-law a stern letter chastising her for her behavior.

Meanwhile, in public appearances, the couple often appeared uncomfortable in each other's company. On a trip to Korea last month, their discomfort was so apparent that reporters took to calling them "the Glums."

Both the Government and the palace appealed to Britain's aggressive tabloid press today to give the Prince and Princess privacy in the coming days, although the news is almost certainly going to increase pressure on the couple from photographers.

In Parliament, Mr. Major's announcement today brought widespread expressions of sympathy. Edward Heath, the former Prime Minister, rose in the Commons to describe Mr. Major's announcement as "one of the saddest made by any Prime Minister in modern times."

But Dennis Skinner, a militant member of the opposition Labor Party who favors abolition of the monarchy, said the royal family had pushed its own "self-destruct button."

"It is high time we stopped this charade of swearing allegiance to the Queen and her heirs and successors, because we don't know from time to time who they are," he said.

To loud cheers, Mr. Major turned to Mr. Skinner and said, "You do not, I believe, speak for the nation or any significant part of it."

Charles and Diana Agree on Divorce Terms

BY SARAH LYALL | JULY 13, 1996

IT BEGAN AS an old-fashioned fairy tale but soon became just another failed modern marriage, brought down by anger, tears and adultery. And today, almost 15 years after the wedding between Lady Diana Spencer and Charles, the Prince of Wales, the consummately incompatible couple announced that they had finally reached an agreement on the terms for their divorce.

Under the agreement, announced in a joint statement by Buckingham Palace, representing Charles, and Anthony Julius, Diana's lawyer, the Princess will receive a big lump-sum payment instead of regular alimony checks. Neither side would release details of the financial settlement, but London newspapers have reported that Diana is getting about $22.5 million in cash, as well as about $600,000 a year earmarked to maintain her private office.

She is to give up her right to be Queen of England and to be called "Her Royal Highness." Queen Elizabeth II was reported to have been ready to allow Diana to retain the honorific, but Prince Charles was said to be adamant that she give it up.

The removal of the "Royal Highness" title, which separates the royal family from the rest of British nobility, officially obliges Diana to curtsy to others who have it — her ex-husband, for instance, and even her own children. But the palace said, rather cryptically, that Princess Diana will continue to be "regarded as a member of the royal family" and "will from time to time receive invitations to state and national public occasions" at the invitation "of the sovereign or the Government."

Diana and Charles, the heir to the British throne, have been formally separated for over three years and have been trying to reach a divorce agreement since February, but negotiations have bogged down in angry demands and counter-demands. Today's statement, though, dismissed in a paragraph all those months of antagonism, asserting that the settlement was "amicable" and had been "greatly assisted by both the fairness of His Royal Highness the Prince of Wales's proposals and by Her Royal Highness the Princess of Wales's ready acceptance of them."

The agreement gives Diana and Charles equal access to their children, Prince William, 14, who is set to succeed his father as King of England, and his brother, Prince Harry, 11. The children spend most of the year at boarding school, and have been alternating holidays with each parent, so there seems little likelihood that the children's lives will be greatly altered.

Diana will also be allowed to keep her apartment at Kensington Palace "with the Queen's agreement," will be given access to the jets used by the royal family, and will, Buckingham Palace said, be able "to use the state apartments at St. James's Palace for entertaining," as long as she asks permission first.

Diana will be forced to vacate her offices next to her ex-husband's at St. James's Palace, but will be allotted space at Kensington Palace for new offices. And although she gets to keep all the jewelry she has amassed during her marriage, she will relinquish — at her own request, Buckingham Palace said — a host of honorary military titles.

It is not clear what would happen if Diana were to remarry, but experts on the royal family believe that she would probably have to relinquish many benefits of the divorce agreement, like her home, the financing of her office and possibly the title "Princess of Wales."

The divorce will not alter Charles's right to become King of England, but if he remarries, Church of England officials have said he might jeopardize his position of supreme governor of the church. However, the Prince has said he has no intention of marrying again.

Today's announcement brings to a sorry end a saga that began with hope and romance more than 15 years ago when Charles, then a somewhat awkward 32-year-old bachelor, announced that he planned to marry the shy Diana, then only 20. But afer a lavish wedding that lifted the spirits of a down-in-the-dumps nation and was eagerly watched by tens of millions of television viewers around the world, relations between the couple began to slide into misunderstanding and hatred.

The couple had few common interests: Charles loved horses, his garden and discussions about philosophy, while the Princess adored fancy clothes, listening to pop music on her Walkman, and telephone gossip. Moreover, it seemed that Charles was still involved with another woman — Camilla Parker Bowles, according to British newspaper reports — and Diana descended into depression and bulimia, making several half-hearted suicide attempts that were widely seen as cries for help.

After a number of years in which the couple's private unhappiness had become clear even in their public appearances, Andrew Morton, one of a legion of British journalists who specialize in the royal family, published "Diana: Her True Story," which revealed all the sordid details of the royal marriage and managed to shatter whatever myths were left. More revelations of mad, bad and bizarre behavior on both sides followed, and in December 1992 the couple announced that they had agreed to a formal separation.

But it wasn't until this winter, after Diana gave an extraordinary television interview in which she described her bulimia and self-mutilation, admitted to adultery and painted a chilling picture of a stiff and uncaring royal family, that Queen Elizabeth, Prince Charles's mother, stepped in and demanded that his son end his marriage.

But even though two of the Queen's other children — Prince Andrew and Princess Anne — have gone through divorces of their own, the end to the Prince of Wales's marriage had no modern precedent. Unlike other couples, the two have hardly been fighting over things like custody of the cat, who has to pay for the childrens' college educations or who gets to keep the Bob Dylan albums.

Instead, the negotiations to end Charles and Diana's marriage have focused on a lump-sum settlement and on what sort of public role Diana — who is far more popular than her reserved husband — would continue to play after the end of her marriage. Conscious that a divorce would chip away her status, Diana has fought to maintain as many of her royal trappings as possible and has pressed for a financial settlement that would allow enable her to maintain her expensive way of living.

In its statement, Buckingham Palace left vague the question of what sort of role Diana might play in the future, saying that would be "essentially for her to decide." However, it said she would have to clear any foreign trips, except those for private vacations, with the Queen (or later, with her ex-husband), and would be allowed to represent the country and the royal family only with the permission of the sovereign and the Government.

And while the financial package is certainly generous (albeit far less than the $75 million she reportedly asked for), Diana has lost a major battle in the requirement that she give up her "Royal Highness" title.

As mother of Prince William, the heir to the throne after his father, Diana is sure to have greater status than her sister-in-law, Sarah, the Duchess of York, who recently concluded her own divorce from the Queen's second son, Prince Andrew.

Harold Brooks-Baker, publishing director of Burke's Peerage and an expert on royal behavior, said that stripping the "H.R.H." from Diana's title was "without historical precedent" and predicted that it would spur a public-opinion backlash.

How a nation that has lapped up every detail of Charles and Diana's courtship, marriage, estrangement and separation will respond to the final chapter in their story together remains to be seen. The palace said the couple's divorce would go to court on Monday, and would be official by the end of August.

It's Official: Charles and Diana Split, and She Pays Her Own Bills

BY SARAH LYALL | AUG. 29, 1996

WITH THE IMPERSONAL THWACK of a rubber stamp, the tumultuous marriage of the Prince and Princess of Wales officially ended today, 15 years after it began.

Their divorce, in the form of a decree absolute in London's High Court, brings to a close a long relationship that started with hope and ceremony and deteriorated into misunderstanding, bitterness and all-out war. Although daily life will probably remain much the same for Prince Charles, the heir to the British throne, there were signs today that the world will change irrevocably for Diana.

For one thing, as of today, she no longer gets to call herself "Her Royal Highness," the title that separates the royal family's inner circle from other nobles, aristocrats and titled hangers-on. Buckingham Palace made her new status quite clear today when it announced that anyone granted an "H.R.H." through marriage would automatically lose it upon divorcing — a category that now applies only to Diana and her sister-in-law, the Duchess of York, who was recently divorced from Charles's brother Andrew.

In addition, the Prince has formally declared that he will no longer foot his ex-wife's bills, leaving her to pay all her expenses out of a lump-sum divorce settlement said to be at least $22.5 million. In a letter signed by Eric Golding, administrator for the couple's settlement, some 40 of the Princess's favorite stores were instructed to begin sending their bills to Diana, not to Charles.

"With effect from 2 September 1996, any expenditure incurred by or on behalf of Her Royal Highness the Princess of Wales, on or after that date should be invoiced directly to the Princess of Wales's Office, Apartment 7, Kensington Palace, London," said the letter, dated Aug. 21 (hence the use of Diana's old title).

The two spent today some 500 miles apart. Diana, 35, was in London, where she had lunch with members of the English National Ballet and was photographed, apparently still wearing her wedding and engagement rings, by paparazzi who had waited all night for a good vantage point. Charles, 47, was with the couple's two sons at Balmoral, the royal family's Scottish estate.

Over the weekend, The News of the World found him spending the weekend with Camilla Parker Bowles, widely regarded in Britain as his longtime mistress, at the home of some mutual friends in Wales. An article, and an accompanying photograph of the two talking to their hosts, were seen in Britain as irrefutable evidence that Charles had continued his reported affair with Mrs. Parker Bowles, whom many Britons blame, at least in part, for the demise of the royal marriage. And they raised anew the questions of whether the Prince plans to remarry, and whether the country is prepared to accept the idea of a Queen Camilla.

A Gallup poll this week suggested that whatever the Prince does, he had better think carefully. A poll of nearly 1,000 church officials and regular churchgoers commissioned by The Daily Telegraph showed that more than half thought that if the Prince remarried — never mind remarrying the unpopular Camilla — he should not be crowned King or made head of the Church of England.

Charles himself has said that he has "no intention of remarrying," at least anytime soon. And Prime Minister John Major himself took up the issue today, telling reporters that remarriage was "purely hypothetical."

"There is no prospect of Prince Charles marrying again at the moment," Mr. Major said. "Maybe at some stage in the future — but that may be some years ahead."

For Media and the Royals, Earl Takes Off His Gloves

BY SARAH LYALL | SEPT. 7, 1997

AMID THE SOOTHING POMP and ceremony of the funeral of Diana, Princess of Wales, the eulogy of her younger brother, Earl Spencer, burst forth yesterday as an undiluted cry of pain and anger.

His tone was respectful and his demeanor composed. But Lord Spencer's searing address at Westminster Abbey was an enormous break with tradition and a stunning indictment of the way his sister had been treated by the two forces that had most influenced the way she lived her final years: the royal family and the news media.

The Earl's remarks were all the more remarkable because, in a sense, he was attacking the royal family in their own church and at a service they had helped plan and were attending as the most distinguished guests. Diana's former in-laws had apparently made peace with her in death. But it was as if the Earl wanted to say that despite this, he had not forgotten the slights she suffered at their hands.

In a direct reference to the Queen's decision last year to strip Diana of the title "Her Royal Highness" as a condition of her divorce from Prince Charles, the heir to the throne, Lord Spencer said his sister was "classless." She had demonstrated since the divorce and her near-ejection from royal status, he said pointedly, "that she needed no royal title to continue to generate her own particular brand of magic."

And he went out of his way to emphasize the differences between Diana's warm, spontaneous, sometimes painfully candid style of living and the royal family's grim adherence to tradition, to duty, to keeping emotions in check rather than expressing them openly.

The Spencers — Diana's "blood family," he called them, making the distinction with the family of her former in-laws — would do their best to help rear her two sons in the way Diana would have wanted, Lord Spencer said.

Addressing his remarks to his dead sister, the Earl said: "We will do all we can to continue the imaginative and loving way in which you were steering these two exceptional young men so that their souls are not simply immersed by duty and tradition, but can sing openly as you planned.

"We fully respect the heritage into which they have both been born and will always respect and encourage them in their royal role. But we, like you, recognize the need for them to experience as many different aspects of life as possible to arm them spiritually and emotionally for the years ahead."

In another startling break with tradition — almost as startling as seeing Elton John singing at such a solemn service and at such a solemn site — some mourners in the Abbey burst into applause after the Earl's remarks. Outside, thousands of people watching on screens set up in Hyde Park were applauding, too; many of them gave the Earl a standing ovation.

The Earl and his two surviving sisters, Lady Sarah McCorquodale and Lady Jane Fellowes, all spoke at the service, as did Prime Minister Tony Blair. But it was significant that no member of the royal family spoke. Nor did any royal family member except Prince Charles, who was accompanying his two sons, attend the Spencer family service on Althorp Estate, where Diana was buried.

Lord Spencer directed his angriest comments at the news media, on which last week he had placed responsibility for Diana's death and which, he said today, "used regularly to drive her to tearful despair." His sister, he said, had seriously considered moving away from Britain "because of the treatment she received at the hands of the newspapers."

"I don't think she ever understood why her genuinely good intentions were sneered at by the media, why there appeared to be a permanent quest on their behalf to bring her down," he said. "It is baffling. My own and only explanation is that genuine goodness is threatening to those at the opposite end of the moral spectrum."

Finally, the Earl spoke warmly and personally of his sister, saying that beyond her beauty and glamor, she was at heart an extremely vulnerable young woman with "deep feelings of unworthiness of which her eating disorders were merely a symptom."

Diana once said on television that her in-laws had never understood her eating problems and that, when it became clear she suffered from bulimia, they had told her she was wasting food. With his remark, Lord Spencer was clearly saying that there were people in Diana's life who had cared about her vulnerabilities — but that the family of her former husband had not been among them.

For Charles, Camilla and Britain, the Wait Is Over

BY SARAH LYALL | APRIL 9, 2005

LONDON, APRIL 8 — Maybe we already know enough about Saturday's royal wedding. But the details have been so complicated, the last-minute adjustments so harrowing, the sense of doom over the whole thing so ominous, that it is worth reviewing a few outstanding items.

Given that Prince Charles and Camilla Parker Bowles have been lovers, on and off, for more than 30 years — a good portion of which they were each married to another person, a question immediately arises: are they sorry for committing adultery?

Well, it might seem so.

The couple plan to follow their wedding ceremony with a religious blessing, a centerpiece of which will be a stern prayer of penitence from the 1662 Book of Common Prayer. The prayer, which they and their 800-odd guests will recite en masse before the archbishop of Canterbury, begins:

"We acknowledge and bewail our manifold sins and wickedness, which we, from time to time, most grievously have committed, by thought, word and deed, against thy Divine Majesty, provoking most justly thy wrath and indignation against us."

If the combined admitted wickedness of 800 guests seems a lot, it's worth remembering that Charles and Camilla know a lot of people. Their eclectic guest list includes the king of Bahrain, the governor-general of Papua New Guinea, the British prime minister, the actor Kenneth Branagh, Camilla's ex-husband, several of Charles's ex-girlfriends, the writer John Mortimer, the comedian Joan Rivers, assorted courtiers and hangers-on, including someone whose official title is "master of the horse."

And, of course, there are Charles's parents, who will be there — although not for the whole thing.

The queen and her husband are staying away from the small civil ceremony, which is to take place at the Guildhall in Windsor with two dozen members of Charles and Camilla's families in attendance. But they and everyone else will go to the religious blessing afterward, at St. George's Chapel in Windsor Castle.

Charles's parents will also be at the reception, in Windsor Castle as well, at which drinks and canapés will be served. But there will be no sit-down dinner, as Charles had hoped.

After the party is over, there may still be some confusion over Camilla's new royal title. In fact, the haggling over it could well last for years. Charles's bride has declared her intention to be known as Her Royal Highness, the Duchess of Cornwall (Charles is the Duke of Cornwall, among other things), and then to become the princess consort upon Charles's accession to the throne.

But some constitutional experts say that, like it or not, she will officially become the Princess of Wales when she marries Charles. Furthermore, they say, under current law, she will automatically become queen when Charles becomes king.

The truth is that no one really seems to know. As a spokesman for the prime minister said when all this came up: "The position at the moment is limited to what the title would be on her marriage. In terms of any future events, let's wait until future events arise."

Fat chance of the ravening news media waiting around for anything. It's been some time since Britain's news organizations deferred to the royal family, and their feelings of antipathy are returned: Charles, especially, hates journalists, boasting to friends about never reading the newspapers or watching the news.

Last week, Britons were amused to see the future king lose it on the ski slopes during an arranged photo opportunity. Blustering in an annoyed fashion, he referred to the assembled royal press pack as "bloody people" and singled out the BBC royal correspondent, Nicholas Witchell, for particular opprobrium.

"I can't bear that man," Charles said. "I mean he's so awful, he really is. I hate these people."

Camilla, on the other hand, has generally kept her head down, enduring stoically and quietly all the unkind things the British tabloids have written about her over the years. In recent days, there have been tiny hints of a slight thaw in the media's temperature.

In a documentary broadcast on ITV on Thursday night, friends like the novelist Jilly Cooper testified to her kindness, loyalty and sense of fun.

In The Times of London on Friday, the broadcaster Jonathan Dimbleby, who wrote an admiring biography of Prince Charles, called Mrs. Parker Bowles "a genuine star."

And The Evening Standard, which has done as much as anyone to prop up the image of the late Diana, Princess of Wales as a saintly figure, took a warmer line in an editorial.

Charles and Camilla deserve "sympathy and respect," it said. "Tomorrow's legitimation of their mutual love and dependence deserves bouquets, not brickbats."

A nice sentiment, that.

But Britain is in the grip of a cold snap and Saturday's weather forecast, sadly, calls for rain.

Britons Strike Sour Notes on Royal Wedding

BY SARAH LYALL | FEB. 18, 2005

LONDON, FEB. 17 — It was, perhaps, inevitable.

In a country that can argue endlessly about such royal minutiae as whether it is appropriate for the queen to keep her breakfast cereal in plastic containers, a backlash against the second marriage of Charles, the Prince of Wales, is well under way.

Whether the couple will win acceptance with their subjects remains to be seen. But one thing is certain: for Charles, it will not be anything like the first time.

"Boring Old Gits to Wed" was how The Star announced the news last week — the other "old git" in the headline being Charles's fiancée, Camilla Parker Bowles. "What is there to celebrate?" asked Amanda Platell in The Daily Mail. "That a 56-year-old man has finally married his mistress?"

Britons have various reasons for their misgivings about the wedding, which is to take place April 8. Some feel that Charles, who cheated on his first wife, Diana, with Mrs. Parker Bowles, does not deserve to live happily ever after with the woman they regard as the agent of Diana's distress. Others simply object on general principle to Mrs. Parker Bowles, who has long been cast as the wicked stepmother in the ruined royal fairy tale.

Still others simply wish the royal family would go away and stop bothering everyone.

"Why should these meaningless people be embedded in our national imagination?" wrote Polly Toynbee, a columnist with The Guardian. "Ludicrous and grotesque for the wretched royal performers and their subjects alike, this is the least dignified of all state institutions."

Certainly all the speculation about Charles's mother, Queen Elizabeth, and her meddlesome attitude toward the wedding has been extremely undignified.

At first the queen seemed almost giddy with joy, at least by her modest emotional standards. "We're very happy," her office said in a statement on the day the engagement was announced. But since then, the queen has appeared intent — if you believe the popular press — on controlling the wedding plans, even if it means overriding her son's wishes.

In normal family weddings, the role of older-generation wedding irritant is rightfully claimed by the mother of the bride, who exercises her natural-born duty to challenge everything from the size of the guest list to the color of the trim on the bridesmaids' sashes. But this is not a normal family, and the queen — who is to be host at the reception, at Windsor Castle — outranks anyone she feels like outranking.

According to Trevor Kavanagh, The Sun's political editor and a man as knowledgeable as anyone when it comes to these matters (which isn't saying a lot), Elizabeth has nixed Charles's idea of having a romantic reception at "dozens of intimate candlelit round tables." Instead, The Sun reported, she wants a muted, stuffy dinner at "one long, formal rectangular table."

More alarmingly for a couple who between them have lived 113 years and produced four children (with other people), the queen has also apparently instituted what The Sun calls a "pre-wedding sex ban," decreeing that they should spend the night before the wedding sleeping "in different wings of the castle." She has also exerted her monarchical prerogative over the menu, Mr. Kavanagh reported, airily dictating that Charles "won't be able to serve dinner guests his beloved organic vegetables from Highgrove."

Whatever her issues with organic produce, at least the queen is resigned to the marriage on the ground that having her son safely wed would remove some of the awkwardness surrounding his relationship with Mrs. Parker Bowles. But others are not happy. No sooner had the engagement been announced than a motley parade of constitutional experts and royal protocol-watchers emerged from the woodwork to provide various reasons the marriage could not, or should not, take place.

There was much talk of the precedent, of tradition and of the 1836 Marriage Act, which according to Stephen Cretney, emeritus professor of legal history at Oxford, could well make their planned civil marriage illegal. The act, which legalized nonchurch weddings for the first time, "does not apply to members of the royal family," he told the BBC.

In an indication of the difficulty of the arrangements, Prince Charles's office announced Thursday that the wedding would be moved to the Guildhall in Windsor, saying that licensing the castle itself for the wedding would be too disruptive.

Then, there was the question of Camilla's status. Not making her queen, argued the historian Andrew Roberts, was "an insult to Camilla and British women." At the other end of the argument was the nagging fear of what an Express headline darkly called the "Queen Camilla Plan," which Charles is said to be plotting to make Camilla queen, even though he said he would not.

The theory goes that the engagement announcement used the word "intended" when saying Camilla would eventually become the princess consort — not the queen — as a sneaky rhetorical way of providing a future escape hatch. As The Express pointed out, the prince had publicly declared several times that that he had "no intention" of remarrying — and look what he is doing now.

Ultimately the issue comes back to Charles and Camilla Parker Bowles, and whether people like them or not. The jury is out on this matter. Unfortunately for the couple, news reports about the engagement have invariably rehearsed, in grisly detail, less-than-proud moments from their shared history: the way she is said to have orchestrated Charles's marriage to Diana because she thought (wrongly) that Diana would prove pliable and clueless; the way he grandly informed Diana that he did not intend to be the only Prince of Wales in history not to have a mistress.

Worst of all was the publication in 1993 of a bugged 11-minute telephone conversation the couple had had when both were married to other people (Charles and Diana separated in 1992). In it was intimate talk of the most excruciating kind, culminating in Charles's distinctly un-regal wish to live, he said, inside his mistress's trousers.

"It was all deeply humiliating," Elizabeth Grice wrote in The Daily Telegraph, in an appraisal of the couple's chances of gaining public acceptance. "None of the dignity that has accrued to them since, through time and patience and good works, will entirely obliterate some of these images."

Charles and Camilla, Married at Last, and With Hardly a Hitch

BY SARAH LYALL | **APRIL 10, 2005**

WINDSOR, ENGLAND, APRIL 9 — Given all the twists of fate and circumstance that have conspired against it, perhaps the most wondrous thing about the wedding on Saturday between Prince Charles and Camilla Parker Bowles is that it took place at all.

But it did, and nothing went wrong. On Saturday, after more than 30 star-crossed years, through other marriages, bitter divorces, violent public opprobrium and familial disapproval, Charles and Camilla finally married.

When the couple emerged, arm in arm, from their civil wedding service at the Guildhall in the middle of this Berkshire town west of London, Camilla had become not only the wife of the heir to the British throne, but also a bona fide member of the royal family. Hereafter, the former Mrs. Parker Bowles will be known officially as Her Royal Highness, the Duchess of Cornwall (unless she becomes queen, which she has said she does not want to do).

The crowds here on Saturday were estimated at about 20,000 people, nothing like the 600,000 that turned out on that long-ago day when Charles married Lady Diana Spencer and, for the briefest of periods, it seemed as if fairy tales really could come true — until it became clear that they could not.

This was different, but not in a bad way. If there was a general mood in the ether during the long afternoon, which included a blessing of the wedding at St. George's Chapel in Windsor Castle, it was one of sympathy for the realistic intimacy of middle-aged love, and a recognition of its differences from the heady but often unknowing love of youth.

"When these vows are made by people who have been battered by life, they somehow have more force and impact than when they are made by people in their 20's, when it's easier to say such things," the novelist Robert Harris told The Daily Telegraph, which in a fit of promonarchical spirit on Saturday printed a page full of tributes to Charles and Camilla from various friends.

Ann Fitzpatrick, who had come to Windsor to stand by the side of the road in hopes of catching a glimpse of the newly married couple, said that she was not particularly fond of the monarchy or even of Prince Charles, but that she wanted to show her support for late-in-life marriage.

"You go through it with more maturity, and not as much ignorance," said Ms. Fitzpatrick, 47. (She herself is hoping to marry her longtime partner, the father of her two children, she said, and maybe Charles's wedding will help nudge him along.) "They've had so many problems," Ms. Fitzpatrick said of the royal couple. "They're not aiming at perfection; just happiness."

The contrast to the prince's first wedding could hardly have been more stark. The first time, Charles was an inexperienced 32-year-old and his bride was a sheltered 20-year-old who had no idea what she was getting into. This time, he is 56, his wife is 57, and they have been around the block and back. Each has married and divorced, and each has two children, all of whom attended the civil ceremony. (Prince William, nervously checking the pocket of his waistcoat for the rings as he went into the Guildhall, served as best man.)

In the wedding 24 years ago, Diana was all but swallowed up by her huge, frothy, meringue-like extravaganza of a dress, with sleeves that puffed out like cotton candy and a train that seemed to go on forever. For his part, the groom wore a foppishly elaborate military uniform, complete with a sword.

This time around, the bride was in an elegant cream suit and broad-brimmed hat, and the groom wore the sort of smart morning suit that makes even the most unprepossessing Englishman look dashing. Suddenly, Mr. Awkward began to seem like Mr. Darcy.

Despite all the Keystone Kops missteps that marred the wedding preparations, including changes to the time and place of the ceremony and the uncomfortable news that Queen Elizabeth would stay away from the Guildhall, attending only the church blessing, everything seemed to go smoothly.

The couple's guests at the civil ceremony — two dozen assorted siblings, children, nieces and nephews — arrived in two buses. Prince William did not lose the wedding rings. Prince Harry, who is said (though by the salacious British tabloids) to resent his new stepmother and who will not soon be allowed to forget his Nazi-outfit gaffe, chatted and joked with his brother.

After the civil ceremony was over, the couple slipped into a Rolls-Royce borrowed from the queen for the short trip up the hill to Windsor Castle, which looms over the town. There they joined some 800 people — including Charles's parents — for the blessing of the marriage, led by the archbishop of Canterbury, the Most Rev. Rowan Williams.

The guests included politicians, the prime minister, Tony Blair, and the leader of the Conservative Party, Michael Howard, among them. There were members of other royal families, like the crown prince and princess of Yugoslavia (which is not a monarchy any more, but never mind), and Prince Bandar bin Sultan of Saudi Arabia.

There was also a collection of actors, including Rowan Atkinson, Kenneth Branagh, Stephen Fry, Joanna Lumley and Timothy West, who read a selection from Wordsworth's "Ode on Intimations of Immortality," with its apt line about "first affections."

Also in the crowd was Camilla's first husband, Andrew Parker Bowles, who is sometimes described as "the man who lay down his wife for the country" on account of Camilla's long affair with Charles during her marriage. He is said (by the BBC) to have telephoned his ex-wife a few days ago to wish her well.

The fancier the wedding, the more outlandish the hats, and there were some winners on Saturday. Writing a contemporaneous Internet Web log as the day went on, Anna Pickard of the newspaper The Guardian reported that the hat of Trudie Styler, Sting's wife, "looked like the sort of thing you could train hamsters to jump through." Meanwhile,

Ms. Pickard reported, Sophie, Countess of Wessex, "seems to be wearing what from this angle looks like an upturned galvanized bucket."

At the religious service, as expected, the couple said they were very sorry for their past mistakes and heartily repented their sins. By now, the new Duchess of Cornwall had changed into a long, swishy dress of silvery blue silk, with a little feather arrangement for a hat. She and her new husband, who had earlier exuded his all-too-familiar look of slightly shifty discomfort, seemed to grow increasingly relaxed and relieved as the day went on.

The couple were openly affectionate during the religious service, lovingly caressing each other's hands. Camilla beamed and Charles looked almost beside himself with joy (by his standards) as they walked down the aisle together.

The queen, following her son and daughter-in-law out the door of St. George's Chapel, seemed determined not to stand next to them. She hovered in back, turned around to talk to other members of the royal family, looked away.

Prince Philip, who is said not to get along with Prince Charles — and who once wrote a letter to Diana expressing his preference for her over Camilla — loomed far off to the side, pointedly leaving a two-person-wide gap between himself and his son's wife.

The two-hour reception featured canapés and the traditional wedding fruitcake.

The couple will make a house party of their honeymoon, with various friends and relations joining them at the prince's estate in Scotland.

With the new, pro-Charles-and-Camilla mood in the air, even Piers Morgan, the cynical former editor of The Daily Mirror and a onetime fan and confidant of Diana, Princess of Wales, was moved to enthusiasm for the wedding.

Speaking on the BBC, where he spent the day commenting on the proceedings as if he was watching a soccer game, Mr. Morgan pronounced, "I think this is turning into a great royal occasion."

Spring Wedding

A poem for the royal wedding by Andrew Motion,
Britain's poet laureate.

I took your news outdoors, and strolled a while
In silence on my square of garden-ground
Where I could dim the roar of arguments,
Ignore the scandal-flywheel whirring round,
And hear instead the green fuse in the flower
Ignite, the breeze stretch out a shadow-hand
To ruffle blossom on its sticking points,
The blackbirds sing, and singing take their stand.
I took your news outdoors, and found the Spring
Had honored all its promises to start
Disclosing how the principles of earth
Can make a common purpose with the heart.
The heart which slips and sidles like a stream
Weighed down by winter-wreckage near its source —
But given time, and come the clearing rain,
Breaks loose to revel in its proper course.

Diana's Legacy: A Reshaped Monarchy, A More Emotional U.K.

BY SARAH LYALL | AUG. 30, 2017

AFTER THE DEATH OF DIANA, Princess of Wales, 20 years ago, London felt like a city on the verge of a revolution. Suddenly everything was up for grabs, even the monarchy itself. For a few crazy weeks, this most enduring of institutions looked as if it might actually implode under the weight of so much emotion.

For anyone there at the time, it was as electrifying as it was bewildering. The mood was febrile, angry, reckless. Flowers were piled knee-deep at the gates of the royal palaces; grown men wept openly in the streets; mild-mannered citizens inveighed against the usually blameless queen for what they believed was an inadequate response to a national crisis. Centuries of stiff-upper-lipped repression boiled over in a great howl of collective anguish.

Eventually the public regained its grip, and the monarchy — chastened and battered, but a monarchy nonetheless — endured. But as Britain on Thursday marks the 20th anniversary of Diana's death with commemorations, documentaries and books, a central, if unlikely, piece of her legacy is how she reshaped the monarchy that rejected her, and how she reshaped Britain, too.

Diana in life was a loose cannon, an unpredictable wild card; in death, she had a galvanizing effect. Britain is already a very different place from Diana's era, partly because of a younger generation less enamored with old conventions. But her death also opened a door, for better or worse, for the country to become more emotional and expressive, and more inclined to value gut feeling over expert opinion even in such matters as "Brexit," its vote last year to leave the European Union.

Faced with a clear choice — modernize or die — the monarchy elected to modernize, led by Queen Elizabeth II but bolstered by a new generation of better-adjusted, better-prepared royals.

"The Windsors, whose most perilous moment came at Diana's death, in fact owe their endurance to her example," said Jonathan Freedland, a columnist for The Guardian, a left-leaning newspaper. "The queen is particularly alert to learning lessons from experience, and in this case the lesson was, 'Don't get on the wrong side of public opinion.' "

Diana was glamorous, magnetic, photogenic, mercurial, manipulative and intuitive; media victim and media perpetrator; the Real Princess of Kensington, a reality star before such a thing existed. If she is a less-defining figure to the generation that has grown up since her death, she still is an object of fascination for the generations who were stunned when she died two decades ago, at the age of 36.

"We gossip about her as if she had just left the room," the novelist Hilary Mantel wrote recently in The Guardian.

And so the papers are full of snippets of "news" that have somehow managed to escape public disclosure until now.

A tourist from Ohio emerges from obscurity to claim he was in the tunnel in Paris at the time of the car accident that killed Diana; her boyfriend, Dodi al-Fayed; and their driver, Henri Paul. A Diana-watcher reports that the princess, her identity muted by a voluminous head scarf, regularly visited the grave of the police protection officer whom she loved and who died in what she believed was an "establishment plot," but was really just a motorcycle accident. Diana's "energy healer" reveals that she has heard from Diana recently (from beyond the grave) and that, in case you were wondering, the deceased princess is pro-Brexit.

"She was interested in the referendum and suggested I vote to leave because Britain was really great before the E.U.," the healer, Simone Simmons, told The Daily Star.

Beyond these sorts of details, which help to keep the princess in the public consciousness and to sell tabloid papers, Diana's influence is perhaps most evident in the evolution of the royal family.

During the days after her death, known now as Diana Week, a nation that had always appreciated the monarchy's adherence to tradition was suddenly demanding that it tear up the old rules and learn new ones, right on the spot. "Show Us You Care," The Daily Express said in its emblematic headline, imploring a staid queen, who had never once let down her guard in public, to address the nation and lower all her flags to half-staff, even as every fiber of her deeply conservative being militated against it.

Seriously shocked by what they encountered, the royal family had no choice but to respond.

"The times were changing, and they were not keeping up with the times," Mr. Freedland said of the royal family. "But the truth is, they did manage to modernize."

As an example, Mr. Freedland pointed to the queen's brief, witty appearance in a film for the opening ceremony of the 2012 London Olympics, in which she greeted the actor Daniel Craig in his guise as James Bond and then appeared to parachute with him into Olympic Stadium (the first part was real; the parachuting was done by a stuntwoman).

The new generation — namely Diana's two sons, William and Harry, and William's wife, Kate — has put a youthful, modern (at least by their standards) spin on what it means to be a royal person in 2017. They exude asexual wholesomeness (in the case of William and Kate) and bad-boy cheekiness (in the case of Harry), and give the appearance of working alongside, not in opposition of, public opinion.

They present as both curiously formal — Harry and William in their tailored suits; Kate in her dress-and-hat combos that make her look 20 years older; the royal children's nanny in an amusingly old-fashioned uniform — and relatively normal, considering how not-normal their lives are.

Diana was considered disloyal and unhinged, an unguided missile, when she went on the BBC in 1995 to talk about her emotional distress. ("There were three of us in this marriage, so it was a bit crowded.") In a sign of how much things have changed, William and Harry are marking the anniversary by speaking publicly about their mother — with royal approval.

Her death also marked a turning point in the history of Britons' relationship to their own ids, ushering in an era in which people have new license to express themselves and feelings can weigh more heavily than reason, Mr. Freedland said.

"The reaction to her death is a preview of the Brexit landscape, in which emotion trumps expertise," he said. "It was a shock to people — we didn't think it was part of the British mind-set — and now, after Brexit, you can see there was something growing there, a willingness to give two fingers to the experts." (Instead of using their middle fingers, Britons use what is known as a two-fingered salute.)

Public opinion polls suggest that nobody is particularly fond of Prince Charles, who at 68 is still waiting for his chance to become king. But they also show that the royal family, led by the seemingly indestructible 91-year-old queen, endures as a comforting unifying thread, providing a constitutional underpinning for a nation whose quirks include the fact that it has no written constitution.

"The royal family is key to our constitution," Geordie Greig, editor of The Mail on Sunday, which publishes its share of royal-related articles, said in an email. "It provides a permanent and historical foundation going back more than 1,000 years."

The pomp and circumstance of its spectacles — the weddings of Charles and Diana and of William and Kate; the funeral of Diana — unify the country "with a familial heartbeat that also resonates around the world," he added.

At the very least, the royal family provides a gossipy distraction for a nation fretting about where it belongs and where it is going in this fraught era of Brexit. When is Harry going to propose to his girlfriend, Meghan Markle, and does it matter that she is American, describes herself as mixed race (and is an actress)? How disappointing is it that, at the age of 35, William has already lost much of his hair? How expensive was Kate's sister's very big, very fancy engagement ring?

Not everyone loves the royal family. Clearly anyone who visits Diana's memorial fountain in Kensington Gardens is part of a self-selecting group, hardly a representative sample of public opinion. But a recent stop there showed how Diana, even after all this time, remains part of the conversation.

"I feel bad for Diana, the way they treated her," said Kristina Landgraf, a German tourist. "She was a good person, she was kicked out of the royal family, and tried to have a personal life."

Visitors to Buckingham Palace said that the royal family held a fascination, even for those who are not really a royal family sort of person.

"I'm more of a democracy type, and I don't like that people rule a country because of their blood," said Jochen Jansen, 22, also visiting from Germany. Yet he had come to the palace just the same: "I'm in London, and this is part of the culture of Great Britain," he said.

The conversation turned, inevitably, to Brexit.

"Also the queen and her husband might be nice people," he said. "And I do hope they're in favor of the E.U."

ILIANA MAGRA CONTRIBUTED REPORTING.

CHAPTER 2

Prince William and Kate Middleton

Prince William's marriage to Catherine, or Kate, Middleton is a rare union. Kate Middleton was born to middle-class parents. She is one of few "commoners" to marry into Britain's royal family. Prince William's disregard for status and tradition set a precedent for a more modern monarchy. The public widely viewed the marriage of William and Kate as a source of hope and reparation after the national grief over Charles and Diana's divorce. News coverage of Prince William and Kate's relationship focuses on both the modernization of royalty itself and the birth of royal heirs.

Diana's Ring Seals Prince William's Marriage Plans

BY SARAH LYALL | NOV. 16, 2010

LONDON — Years of fevered anticipation and premature speculation ended on Tuesday morning when Prince William, the heir to the heir to the British throne, said that, yes, he did plan to marry his girlfriend of many years, Kate Middleton.

In a brief statement, William's father, Prince Charles, said that he was "delighted" to announce the engagement of William and Miss Middleton, both 28, and that they would be married next spring or summer.

"Prince William has informed the queen and other close members of his family," the statement said. "Prince William has also sought the permission of Miss Middleton's father."

The statement added that the couple would live in north Wales, where William works as a search-and-rescue helicopter pilot for the Royal Air Force. The announcement ends the long and winding "Will he or won't he?" saga that has provided years of diversion for royal enthusiasts and helped keep the royal-focused gossip industry afloat. It also renders obsolete Miss Middleton's sometime tabloid nickname, "Waity Katie," a reference to the notion that she has supposedly been waiting around for Prince William to propose.

Interested parties can now focus on a new set of pressing issues: Who will design Miss Middleton's wedding dress? Who will be Prince Harry's date at the wedding? And, should Miss Middleton become queen — which would not take place until the death of both the current queen and the future king, Prince Charles — will everyone call her Queen Kate? (Her formal name is Catherine.)

The question of the engagement ring has already been answered. Prince William gave Miss Middleton the sapphire and diamond ring that his father had given his mother — Diana, Princess of Wales — for their engagement in 1981.

At a brief press conference with his arm locked together with his fiancée's, William said that giving Miss Middleton that ring was "my way of making sure my mother didn't miss out on today and the excitement."

"It's very special to me," he said. "As Kate's very special to me now, it was right to put the two together."

Miss Middleton is a different sort of royal bride from Diana, whose short life ended when she was killed after a car accident in Paris in 1997. Diana was naïve and indifferently educated, but she was the daughter of an earl whose family had always mixed in royal circles. By contrast, Miss Middleton, who grew up in Bucklebury, West Berkshire, is considered solidly middle class by British standards.

Her father is a former British Airways officer and her mother a former flight attendant; together, they run a successful mail-order business that sells paraphernalia for children's parties.

By all accounts, Miss Middleton is tough and savvy, and far better equipped to deal with media attention than Diana was. Also, while Charles and Diana hardly knew each other at the time of their engagement, Miss Middleton has been virtually living with Prince William for some time and has met his father many times. The couple became engaged in October during a private holiday in Kenya, Prince Charles's announcement said.

After an autumn of dismaying news about budget cuts and Austerity Britain, the engagement provided an all-purpose happy diversion. The BBC started providing saturation coverage of the announcement. Queen Elizabeth proclaimed herself to be "absolutely delighted." Prime Minister David Cameron said that when he announced the news, members of his cabinet responded with a "great cheer" and "banging of the table." The prime minister also admitted that in 1981 he slept on the street outside Buckingham Palace the night before the wedding of William's parents.

Ed Miliband, leader of the Labour Party, said that he was also delighted, and that "the whole country will be wishing them every happiness."

Prince William and Miss Middleton met at the University of St. Andrews in Scotland, and then shared a group house with two other students. According to news reports, the highlights of their college years together included the time that Miss Middleton persuaded a wavering William not to drop out when he was having a hard time his first year, and the time that she took part in a charity fashion show wearing just her underwear.

(The university said on Tuesday that it was "Britain's top matchmaking university," claiming that 10 percent of its students met the person with whom they would eventually settle down. It invited the couple to visit whenever they wanted.)

Should Miss Middleton become Queen Catherine, she would be the first queen in British history to have a college degree, or indeed, to have any college education at all.

The couple's relationship has had its ups and downs. William and Miss Middleton split for several months in 2007, and there was speculation in the British tabloids (always denied) that the royal family was dismayed by the supposedly déclassé behavior of the Middletons. Miss Middleton's mother, Carole, was said to have chewed gum and used unaristocratic words like "toilet" and "pardon" in front of the queen, and some of William's friends were said to mutter "doors to manual" when Miss Middleton came into the room, a reference to her mother's prior career.

No one ever confirmed those stories, and some royal-watchers pointed out that since Mrs. Middleton did not appear to have yet spoken to the queen at that point, it was highly unlikely that she would have had occasion to say much, let alone use the word "toilet" in the queen's hearing.

The couple gave an interview to ITV later on Tuesday and revealed themselves to be relaxed and playful together. Asked if the rumor that she had a poster of Prince William on her wall when she was a girl was true, Miss Middleton said, "He wishes." (In fact, she added, she had a "Levi's guy" on her wall.)

They talked about how the prince had tried to impress her with his cooking early in their relationship, but that, as he admitted, "I get quite lazy" now. They also joked about their long relationship. ("How many years?" Miss Middleton asked.)

Of the period in which they split up, Miss Middleton said, "I wasn't very happy about it," but added that in retrospect she had valued the time alone.

"Phew," William said.

He said that there was "something very special about her." As for himself, he said, "I'm obviously extremely funny, and she loves that."

Meanwhile, news crews spent the day massed outside London's various royal palaces, interviewing royal experts who speculated on things like where and when the wedding would take place and what kind of charities Miss Middleton would support. The experts did not know much, but they did their best.

Prince William and Kate Middleton pose for photographs in the State Apartments of St. James Palace on November 16, 2010, in London, England. The couple became engaged during a recent holiday in Kenya having been together for eight years.

Ingrid Seward, whose position as editor of the magazine Majesty ("The Quality Royal Magazine") makes her a regular presence at these occasions, said, "For Majesty Magazine, this is absolutely wonderful."

ALAN COWELL CONTRIBUTED REPORTING.

British Royal Wedding Set for April 29

BY SARAH LYALL | NOV. 23, 2010

LONDON — The date and location have been set: the wedding of Prince William and Kate Middleton is to take place on April 29 at Westminster Abbey.

An aide to Prince William said Tuesday that the couple had chosen the abbey, where Queen Elizabeth was also married, for its "staggering beauty" and because it offered intimacy despite its grand scale.

Prime Minister David Cameron has declared April 29, a Friday, a national holiday, meaning that most Britons will get a four-day weekend because that Monday, May 2, is already a holiday.

"We want to mark the day as one of national celebration," Mr. Cameron said. "A public holiday will ensure the most people possible will have a chance to celebrate on the day."

The abbey is a traditional royal wedding site: Queen Elizabeth and the Queen Mother were married there. The funeral of Prince William's mother, Diana, Princess of Wales, was also held there. On that day, Prince William walked behind his mother's coffin as it was carried to the abbey.

"The venue has long associations with the royal family — it is, in many ways, the royal family's church — and, of course, with William personally," Jamie Lowther-Pinkerton, the prince's private secretary, told reporters.

The wedding is to be paid for by the royal family, Mr. Cameron said, although public funds will be used for security and other ancillary costs. With Britain in the throes of its most drastic austerity measures in decades, the royal family seems particularly anxious to avoid the impression that the wedding will add to the public burden.

Mr. Lowther-Pinkerton said that the couple were "calling the shots" on the wedding plans, with a "rather large supporting cast."

"The couple are very, very keen indeed that the spectacle should be a classic example of what Britain does best," he said.

But with British forces deployed in Afghanistan, Prince William — a serving officer in the Royal Air Force — and his bride-to-be were said to be anxious not to draw troops away from front-line duties or training missions for ceremonial purposes.

Mr. Lowther-Pinkerton added, "The couple are very mindful of the current situation, and for example, Prince William has already expressed a clear wish that any involvement by the armed forces should rely in great part on those servicemen and women already committed to public and ceremonial duties."

"I've never seen two happier people," Mr. Lowther-Pinkerton said. "They're on cloud nine, like any other newly engaged couple."

London's great cathedrals are heavily laden with royal history — and mixed memories.

Prince William's parents, Charles and Diana, were married in St. Paul's Cathedral, but that marriage ended 15 years later in divorce, as did three other modern royal weddings at Westminster Abbey in the past half-century. But the marriage of William's grandmother, Queen Elizabeth II, to Prince Philip at Westminster Abbey has endured since 1947.

Six years later, the queen was crowned at the abbey in June 1953, after the death of her father, King George VI, in 1952. That ceremony was closely followed on television, with many Britons clustering around small black-and-white sets to watch the ceremony. The wedding next April is forecast to attract millions around the world, if the interest in Charles and Diana's wedding is any measure.

The site is one that reaches back centuries in monarchic tradition.

"Westminster Abbey is steeped in more than a thousand years of history," the abbey's Web site declares. "Benedictine monks first came to this site in the middle of the 10th century, establishing a tradition of daily worship which continues to this day."

"The abbey has been the coronation church since 1066" — when the Norman King William I was crowned — "and is the final resting place of 17 monarchs."

ALAN COWELL CONTRIBUTED REPORTING FROM PARIS.

Fixating on a Future Royal
as Elusive as Cinderella

BY SARAH LYALL | APRIL 21, 2011

LONDON — The theme of the walking tour was the forthcoming royal wedding, but the object of the group's obsession was Kate Middleton, the royal bride. In Mayfair, the guide paused at the next important landmark: the Jigsaw store on Dover Street.

"Kate's struggle to hold down a job since graduating has reportedly earned the displeasure of the queen," declared the guide, Hana Umezawa, as earnestly as if she were explaining the Spanish Armada. "The closest Kate has come to having a regular job was when she worked at Jigsaw as a part-time assistant accessories buyer from 2006 to 2007."

What do you say about a young woman who went to college, fell in love and became engaged? With Kate and Prince William's wedding a little more than a week away, the chances of the public — that is, us — learning anything new about Miss Middleton before she turns into a princess (or a duchess, depending on which title she takes) are zero.

Now 29, she has formally spoken to the press only on the day she and William announced their engagement and submitted to a gentle sprinkling of softball questions. She appears to have spent a lifetime avoiding unseemly episodes.

"It's absolutely extraordinary — people do comment and talk about what she's like, but we know almost nothing about her," said Valentine Low, who writes about the royal family for The Times of London. "She's a blank cipher. She's existed in this funny little bubble for the past nine years, and they've done a brilliant job of controlling the flow of information, just letting out enough for us to feel that we're getting something."

Miss Middleton is a rarity in this era of lives played out in public: a megacelebrity who has never been on a reality show, has no Facebook page, does not tweet and is not preparing to reveal all in a memoir. She is like an old-time Hollywood star, full of mystery, a canvas onto which the world can project its fantasies.

If Diana, Princess of Wales, was an aristocrat with a common touch, Kate Middleton is a commoner who has triumphed among aristocrats. But just as it did with Diana, a public voracious for new juicy details will have to make do with recycled scraps from a banquet that has long since been served and cleared away.

How she grew up in Bucklebury, Berkshire, with two loving and good-looking parents who met while working at British Airways, he as a flight dispatcher and she as a flight attendant.

How she has a brother, James, who has largely stayed out of the limelight, and a sister, Pippa, who largely hasn't.

How her mother, Carole, has ancestors who were miners, and how Carole left behind her working-class roots when she and Kate's father, Michael, founded a successful Internet business that sells party accessories. How their newfound wealth allowed them to move into a grand country house and to send Kate to Marlborough College, an elite boarding school, where she excelled at sports but not, unfortunately, at misbehaving.

There is some debate over how early Miss Middleton became aware of Prince William as a potential husband. In his book "William and Kate: A Royal Love Story," Christopher Andersen describes her as having spent her teen years fantasizing about William, poring over news articles about him, even putting images of him up on her wall.

Asked in their engagement interview whether she in fact did display a poster of William in her dorm room, Kate grinned and said, "He wishes." (She added: "I had the Levi's guy on my wall — not a picture of William. Sorry.")

Their courtship at the University of St. Andrews, where both were students, has been told in endless articles, books and television specials. But only a few insiders know if the episode that is supposed to have ignited the royal passion — when Kate appeared at a fashion show in a see-through dress and William uttered the prosaic but fateful words, "Wow! Kate's hot!" — really happened that way.

The two, who by all accounts have an easy and joking relationship, lived together in a group house, first as friends and then as a couple. He introduced her to his family and hung out with hers. When he wavered about whether college was right for him, she persuaded him to stay.

They graduated. He joined the military. She worked part time for Jigsaw, and part time for her parents. She stopped working. They went to a lot of nightclubs.

Another key spot on the royal wedding tour was Mahiki, a Polynesian-themed club that is a known drinking location for William, a (possibly reformed) known drinker.

Here, Ms. Umezawa related, William's friends were believed "to treat Kate unkindly by making derogatory references to her middle-class background," including muttering the flight-attendant phrase "doors to manual" when they saw her. It was also here, she said, that William came to celebrate after he and Kate (briefly) broke up in 2007, leaping onto a table, yelling "I'm free," and amassing an $18,000 bar bill in less than a week.

Since they've reconciled — "Kate, by her aloof behavior, gained the upper hand," Ms. Umezawa explained — they have lived together in Anglesey, Wales, where William works as a search-and-rescue pilot for the Royal Air Force. They reportedly do their own shopping and possibly even their own cleaning.

"Kate has played it beautifully," said Kate Reardon, the editor of Tatler magazine. "She appears to be modest and conservative and un-showoffy and everything that we would love her to be."

In her last days being single, Miss Middleton appeared to have gone into lockdown. However, she was spotted shopping in London this week. But the more she stays out of the limelight, the more fevered and, in a way, paltry, the speculation becomes. She designed her own wedding dress! No, she had three competing dresses made by three competing designers! No, she has one dress, and it is locked in a vault in Clarence House (home of Prince Charles)! She is worryingly thin; how will the dress fit?

None of this will be cleared up until the big day. Even Hello!, a magazine that can turn the rustling of a breeze near a royal palace into a news story, has had to make do with less than usual.

"Kate's big wedding secret revealed," it promised on the cover of last week's issue. Inside it disclosed, citing unnamed sources, that Miss Middleton would not hire a professional makeup artist for her wedding but would apply her own.

That seems highly unlikely, given that a television and Internet audience of approximately 2.5 billion people will be on hand next Friday to critique her makeup job, along with everything else about her. And think of the wedding photos.

But who knows? The palace had no comment.

In This Fairy Tale, Not One, but Two Queens in Waiting

BY JOHN F. BURNS | APRIL 18, 2011

LONDON — When 1,900 invited guests take their coveted places in Westminster Abbey next week for the wedding of Prince William and Kate Middleton, one of the most uneasy seats in the 13th-century Gothic church may be the one occupied by Camilla, Duchess of Cornwall, the longtime lover of Prince Charles, and since her marriage to the heir to the throne in 2005, the stepmother to William, Charles's older son.

One of the most compelling themes of the April 29 wedding will be Britain's odd-couple pair of "queens-in-waiting," Ms. Middleton and Camilla. Though more than 30 years apart in age, both have come to their marriages as what are known in Britain as commoners, and stand, on their husbands' ascent to the throne — Camilla first, and later Kate — to take their places as the highest-placed women in the land.

There, mostly, the similarities end.

Kate, glamorous and young — 29, five months older than Prince William — is seen by many in Britain, along with her future husband, as the potential savior of a monarchy whose luster has been deeply tarnished in the past 30 years.

For all the public acclaim for Queen Elizabeth II, who turns 85 this week and celebrates her 60th anniversary as monarch next year, the story of the other members of the royal family has been one of serial divorces, personal indiscretions, extravagance at taxpayers' expense and suspicious financial dealings that have made lurid copy for Britain's tabloid press.

Camilla, once cast by the tabloids as the most hated woman in the country for her role in dooming Prince Charles's marriage to Diana, Princess of Wales, has gone some distance toward redeeming herself in recent years, to judge by polls that show sharply reduced levels of personal antipathy toward her.

She has been embraced by Diana's two sons, William and Harry, who have said publicly that they love her, not least for the happiness she had brought their father.

The sense of her having achieved insider status in the family, at least with the younger generation, was enhanced when she was photographed this year emerging from a tête-à-tête lunch with Kate in a London restaurant, where she was overheard amid peals of laughter urging the bride-to-be to follow royal tradition — and Diana's precedent — by wearing a jeweled tiara at the wedding, something Ms. Middleton apparently thought was too fusty for her taste.

But the process of rehabilitation appears to have advanced nowhere near enough — at least not yet — for Camilla, 63, to overcome the widespread opposition polls have shown to her ever being formally proclaimed queen if, and when, Charles, 62, becomes king.

For years, the polls have shown 50 to 60 percent of those surveyed in favor of skipping a generation in the succession, relegating Charles and Camilla to a leisured country retirement and jumping straight to William and Kate while they are still relatively young.

Partly, the polls reflect a concern that Charles may be too old to become king — in his 70s, perhaps even his 80s — if his mother lives as long as her mother, Queen Elizabeth the Queen Mother, who died at the age of 101 in 2002. Already, he is seen as a fogy, with his passion for double-breasted suits on occasions that cry out for something more casual, and an awkward personal manner that can incline to the pompous and patronizing.

But the problem is not Charles's alone. The polls that show a majority favoring his stepping aside in William's favor after Queen Elizabeth dies have captured only anemic levels of support — 14 percent in a Harris poll last November — for Camilla's becoming queen even if Charles does succeed his mother.

Against this background — and the hints of a possible constitutional crisis that it carries — the wedding has emerged partly as a story of reconciliation, a stage for the royal family to showcase how far they have progressed in healing the wounds of the past.

What more striking demonstration of that could there be than the sight of Camilla seated in the abbey only a few places from the queen, who is said to have described her at the height of the turmoil over Charles and Diana as "that wicked woman"?

Friends of Camilla's interviewed for this article say the public resistance is deeply unfair to a woman who has put barely a foot wrong since marrying Charles.

From the start, they say, she and Charles understood that winning public acceptance would be a lengthy process — "the pursuit of a gradual acquiescence," as one friend put it. One acknowledgment of that came with Camilla taking her titles, Duchess of Cornwall in England and Duchess of Rothesay in Scotland, from Charles's lesser entitlements, instead of Princess of Wales, the normal title for the wife of the next in line to the throne.

Another was Buckingham Palace's announcement on the occasion of the couple's marriage in 2005 that Camilla would take the title of princess consort, not queen, when Charles takes the throne.

Friends say that one of Camilla's strengths has been the stoicism with which she has borne the wounding barbs thrown at her by an unfriendly press which, like much of the public, remains wedded to an iconic image of Diana despite some of the unflattering revelations that have emerged about her since her death in a Paris car crash in 1997.

The newspaper The Observer once described Camilla as "an older woman with no dress sense and bird's nest hair," while other newspaper critics have said she "packs the stylistic punch of a Yorkshire pudding," and have described her variously as an "old boiler," "old trout," "hatchet face" and "frump."

Her resilience has been leavened with self-deprecating humor. She has made fun of Diana's embittered nickname for her, answering the telephone at her country home west of London, "Rottweiler here!" She has never disguised her fondness for a drink, though she gave up a

Commemorative playing cards depicting the royal family at the Museum of Brands, Packaging and Advertising in London.

30-cigarette-a-day smoking habit at the insistence of Charles. After her first, long-delayed meeting with Prince William, in 1998, she is said to have turned to a friend in relief, saying, "I really need a gin and tonic.

"Friends note, too, that while she has a reputation for holding strong and often unfashionable views, and an impatience with pomposity or pretension, she has been unusually successful in this generation of royals in not bleeding those views into the public domain.

Above all, friends say, she has resisted the temptation to offer a public riposte or even the mildest self-defense against her detractors, as Charles and Diana did by confiding in biographers and television interviewers as their marriage disintegrated.

In a country that holds a special contempt for whingers — those inclined to incessant complaint, a shortcoming many have discerned in Prince Charles — she has won praise for what one of her biographers, Rebecca Tyrrel, describes as an attitude of "You just bloody well get on with it."

That view finds wide support. "She's done a lot in a quiet way," said William Shawcross, an author and journalist who was a childhood friend of Camilla's in the rolling hills of West Sussex. "She has grown into her role in a steady and wise manner."

In practice, the potential situations that favor Charles's giving way to his son, or taking the throne as king without Camilla as his queen, seem likely to collide with political and constitutional reality.

For one thing, the royal family has an established aversion to the idea of abdication. King Edward VIII's decision to quit the throne in 1936 to marry Wallis Simpson remains a grim shadow in the royal memory, especially for Queen Elizabeth, who is said to remain haunted by the trauma her father, King George VI, suffered when he was forced to take the throne.

In an interview for this article, Richard Drayton, a professor of history at King's College, London, said that bypassing Charles would face forbidding obstacles, including "an act of Parliament, and probably a decision by Charles himself to abdicate."

Constitutional experts have said that nothing in Britain's constitutional tradition or common law provides for the wife of the king's not becoming queen, and that Camilla would, in practice, be Britain's queen, whatever title she carried.

How much Camilla cares is a matter of debate. Some of her friends believe her concern is mostly for Charles, who has always said that he sees it as his destiny to become king, and has worked restlessly to that end, with a schedule of public duties that far outstrip any other royal family member, including his mother. Others say Camilla herself is not as come-what-may about the issue as she has sometimes suggested to friends, and would like one day to be back in the abbey, seated beside Charles, as crowns are placed on their heads.

Twice in recent months, the couple has hinted that they remain hopeful of turning the tide of public favor their way on the issue of

Camilla's becoming queen. In an interview in November with Brian Williams of NBC, Charles answered hopefully when asked whether Camilla would ever be the queen. "You know, I mean, we'll see," he replied, as if ambushed by the question. "That could be."

In February, it was Camilla's turn. "Are you going to be queen one day?" a little girl asked her on a visit to a children's center in the Wiltshire town of Chippenham. "You never know," Camilla replied, smiling.

RAVI SOMAIYA CONTRIBUTED REPORTING.

Royals Show Little Affinity for Rank as They Take Spouses

BY SUZY MENKES | NOV. 16, 2010

PARIS — The Facebook page looks like any other — give or take a fancy royal crest. But the father happens to be Prince Charles, who put out a simple online announcement that William, his son, is to marry his long-term partner, Miss Catherine Middleton, less formally known as Kate.

The news of the long-expected engagement of Prince William of Wales spread across the blogosphere on Tuesday in a way unimaginable even when the couple first met at college seven years ago.

Anyone and everyone can now pronounce on Twitter an opinion on the first "middle class" bride to be added to a roster of princesses who once were chosen from a bloodline as distinguished as those of Queen Elizabeth's horses.

For this first mega-royal marriage of the digital age, the British royal family, still bruised by the disastrous marriage and tragic end of Princess Diana, William's mother, will want to make the forthcoming nuptials as inclusive as possible.

However grand the reality of life in a royal palace (although William and Kate will set up home in Wales, near the prince's air force headquarters) the wedding cannot be seen as an exclusive, aristocratic affair.

And so it is across Europe, where royal princes — or a rare crown princess — have married partners of choice, to bring a fresh spirit and to link the royal heritage more closely to its people.

Everything that Ms. Middleton has done so far has been an example of what once would have been called "good breeding." In spite of joining the upper crust set of William and his wilder, younger brother, Harry, the graceful young woman has never been spotted rolling out of a night club in disarray. And even though she is now 28, she does not appear to have what the tabloid press discreetly call "a past."

European royalty of the new generation has entirely broken the system of rank and class, established when a cousinhood of royal children created a spider's web of alliances.

As Colombe Pringle, editor of Point de Vue, France's royal "bible," says: "Before there were arranged, dynastic marriages, but they would not be accepted by the world, so marriages are for love."

The last royal wedding to have drawn a troop of tiaras was Crown Princess Victoria of Sweden, who was married in June to her former fitness trainer Daniel Westling.

Next up — although probably after the Kate/William nuptials — will be Prince Albert of Monaco, who, at age 52, will marry next summer Charlene Wittstock, a South African-born professional swimmer. With her classic, blonde beauty, Ms. Wittstock has the task of stepping into the slippers of the late Princess Grace, the Hollywood star who epitomized a new royal era of glamour and celebrity.

Do these marriages of smart commoners work well in a world where most of their subjects may not care too much and royal aficionados are quick to criticize any supposed breaches of protocol? The withdrawal from public life of the troubled Crown Princess Masako of Japan proves that not every fresh, intelligent arrival into a royal dynasty is successful.

The trials and tribulations of Princess Letizia of Spain, a former television presenter married to Felipe, heir to the Spanish throne, have been splashed over Point de Vue, which has discussed Letizia's supposed rupture with the born-royal Infantas — her sisters-in-law.

But Ms. Pringle says that the idea of a prince marrying an ambitious, organized businesswoman, like the Australian Mary of Denmark or the Argentine-born Maxima, wife of the heir to the Dutch throne, is a reflection of modern times — and that her readers even see it as a feminist update of the Cinderella fairy tale.

For Hugo Vickers, a royal author whose books have included a biography of Elizabeth, the Queen Mother, great-grandmother to William, the Windsor dynasty has frequently brought in fresh blood. (Prince

Charles's own brothers and sister all married outside royal and aristocratic circles.) And for those who want a little back history on the Middleton family, Mr. Vickers has traced its origins to 1240.

"The main thing is that they are a young couple who have grown up together, when he hadn't a lot of self-confidence," said Mr. Vickers on the subject of William and Kate. "People have said rather rude things about her and her family, but they have behaved with poise and dignity."

Ms. Middleton has also kept out of the limelight. As Mr. Vickers points out, until the announcement Tuesday, her voice had never been heard in public. Her ability to reverse the trend toward celebrity overkill, introduced in the Diana years, is one of the reasons that the impeccable Ms. Middleton seems well-equipped to reboot the royal image.

A Traditional Royal Wedding, but for the 3 Billion Witnesses

BY SARAH LYALL | APRIL 29, 2011

LONDON — In the end, Friday's wedding between Prince William and Kate Middleton may not have ushered in a new dawn for the frayed royal family or brought a renewed era of optimism to a country beset by financial woes, as some predicted in the overheated countdown to the big day. But it proved that the British still know how to combine pageantry, solemnity and romance (and wild hats) better than anyone else in the world.

It was an impeccably choreographed occasion of high pomp and heartfelt emotion, of ancient customs tweaked by modern developments (Elton John brought his husband).

Viewing estimates for the ceremony, at 11 a.m. British time on the dot, hovered in the three billion range, give or take 500 million. Australians

ANWAR HUSSEIN/WIREIMAGE

Prince William, Duke of Cambridge, and Catherine Middleton, Duchess of Cambridge, kiss on the balcony of Buckingham Palace following their wedding on April 29, 2011.

held bouquet-throwing competitions; people in Hong Kong wore Kate and William masks; New Yorkers rose by dawn to watch the entrance of guests like Victoria Beckham, teetering pregnantly in sky-high Christian Louboutin heels, Guy Ritchie, the former Mr. Madonna, and assorted monarchs from European countries that are no longer monarchies, like Bulgaria.

In London, the Metropolitan Police said, a million people lined the route of the royal procession, and half a million gathered in front of Buckingham Palace to watch the bride and groom, now known as the Duke and Duchess of Cambridge, kiss (twice) on the palace balcony.

People paid attention almost despite themselves.

"I never really think too seriously about them," said Kathy Gunn, 54, speaking of the royal family. Yet she had somehow been inexorably sucked into the spirit of the occasion, watching it unfold with a crowd on a huge screen at a cafe in central London. "It gives you a great sense of community and spirit," she said. "I am a royalist for the day."

In a world of scattered attention, the occasion had the effect of providing a single international conversation about a subject with universal appeal. It was like a party scene in "Dallas," only with Prince Philip instead of J. R. Ewing.

Grizzled political correspondents, hauled in to television studios to serve as wedding anchors, found themselves talking in all seriousness about the passementerie of the mother of the bride's dress and the provenance of Miss Middleton's tiara. (She borrowed it from Queen Elizabeth, in case you were wondering. It is made of a great many diamonds.)

There was a feast of interesting particulars. First, Kate's dress. Though The Daily Mail successfully predicted the name of the designer — Sarah Burton at Alexander McQueen — it was still an official secret, so much so that Ms. Burton tried to sneak into Kate's hotel on Thursday night with her face mostly obscured by a huge yeti-like fur hat.

St. James's Palace released the details of the dress just as Miss Middleton stepped out of a royal Rolls-Royce with her father, Michael, to walk down the aisle at Westminster Abbey.

Her "something old" was the design of the dress, using traditional craftsmanship. "Something new" was represented by her earrings, a gift from her parents. The tiara was borrowed, and she had a blue ribbon sewn into her dress for her blue item.

Prince William wore the bright scarlet coat of an Irish Guards mounted officer, the uniform of his senior honorary army appointment. He was wearing "gold sword slings," St. James's Palace said, but no sword.

The outfits of the guests were generally tasteful and royal-friendly. A few things stuck out. The exotic costumes of foreign dignitaries, seeming throwbacks to imperial times. The hats worn by the ladies, which resembled, variously, overturned buckets, flowerpots, lampshades, fezzes, salad plates, tea cozies, flying saucers, abstract artworks or, in one case, a pile of feathers. There were also a number of fascinators, decorative shapes with flowers or feathers, that are stuck in one's hair but are not hats.

Catty observers pointed out that Prime Minister David Cameron's wife, Samantha, was possibly the only female guest who wore no hat (or fascinator) at all.

Mr. Cameron wore a traditional morning suit. The dress code had filled him with angst this month when news broke out that in order to avoid appearing too posh, he intended to wear a regular business suit, what the British call a "lounge suit." But as scorn poured upon him — he is in fact posh and frequently wears posh clothes — he said that he would wear a morning suit after all.

Some questions were also raised about the guest list. John Major and Margaret Thatcher, former Conservative prime ministers, were invited; Tony Blair and Gordon Brown, former Labour prime ministers, were not. (Mr. Major attended; Lady Thatcher was ill and stayed home.) The Syrian ambassador was invited, and then uninvited. Sarah Ferguson, the Duchess of York, was never invited.

The new duchess, of course, has parents who made their own fortune with an Internet party-accouterments business. Even a generation ago, she would have been considered unthinkable as a prospective royal bride.

The country's merciless news media have been watching hopefully, and mostly fruitlessly, for signs of middle-class behavior from the Middletons. One TV commentator, standing outside the Goring Hotel, which the Middletons rented for the night before the wedding, remarked, "It's sometimes hard to tell who are Middletons and who are staff."

But except for having no titles, no inherited tiaras and no military uniforms, the Middletons were indistinguishable from the guests at the wedding. The bride's mother, Carole, wore a lovely outfit by Catherine Walker, an aristocrat-approved designer; she did not chew gum, as she was said to have done once when she appeared in public at a royal event, or exhibit déclassé tendencies of any kind.

Kate's elevation, such as it is, to royalty adds a special frisson to the story of her romance with William. The world knows that there are often no fairy-tale endings to these made-for-television moments — the collapse of the marriage of William's parents being the most obvious example. But this couple seems to be a real one, with the potential to resuscitate the image of a royal family tarnished by misadventures like the antics of Prince Harry and Prince Andrew, and resentment over privilege and expenditures.

Kate, who promised to love William but not to obey him, is not actually a princess yet (if she were, she would be called Princess William, which is perhaps not a dream title). But she seems already at ease in what will now be a lifetime job, one with a heavy burden of responsibility as well as great privilege. As the couple drove in their horse-drawn carriage from the church to Buckingham Palace, she waved like a pro — from the wrist, the royal way.

RAVI SOMAIYA CONTRIBUTED REPORTING.

Passion Versus Pageantry in Royal Wedding Reports

BY ALESSANDRA STANLEY | APRIL 29, 2011

The kiss was really not much more than a peck.

Prince William's balcony clinch with his bride, Kate Middleton, was so quick and perfunctory that the CBS anchor Katie Couric missed it and asked for an instant replay. And another. "I hate to be ungrateful," Ms. Couric said on Friday morning. "But is that it?"

The "Today" show on NBC, which had rather crassly plastered a kiss countdown clock on the screen, was just as let down and replayed the royal smooch in gauzy slow motion. CNN's Piers Morgan, who had predicted that it would "go down in history as one of the great kisses," had to eat crow when the disappointed crowds outside Buckingham

BY ASHLEY GILBERTSON FOR THE NEW YORK TIMES

British coverage of the royal wedding emphasized tradition but American broadcasters focused more on the relationship between Prince William and Kate Middleton. Above, a British tourist watches the wedding in Times Square.

Palace demanded a do-over. He had to eat crow again after he assured his co-hosts that Prince William would do no such thing.

"You don't understand the royals," he said loftily, moments before the groom bent down for a second, but still far from ardent, try. The BBC, on the other hand, was perfectly satisfied.

And more than anything else, those clashing kiss expectations are what separated British and American coverage of the royal wedding. On BBC America, which carried the live BBC feed, the anchor Huw Edwards emphasized tradition and continuity. American television craves change. The embrace on the balcony was supposed to be passionate and juicy, a video confirmation of the narrative built into almost all the American coverage, namely that this royal union is a do-over for the one between Prince Charles and Diana Spencer in 1981 that was presented as a gossamer fairy tale and turned out to be a horror story.

This time, according to almost every anchor and commentator, it's a real love match. But the first public embrace, which looked, as the Tudor historian David Starkey put it on CBS, like "an old married couple's kiss" didn't fit the image. For one thing, it wasn't any more smoldering than the brief kiss Prince Charles gave his bride 30 years ago.

Barbara Walters on ABC supplied a better spin. "But you know they talk to each other, they laugh together, you feel the emotion between them," she said. "And looking back at Princess Diana and Prince Charles, you did not feel that."

ABC's coverage evoked other royal memories. The network put Diane Sawyer and Barbara Walters side by side in what looked like an anchor-booth version of the old Princess Diana and Camilla Parker Bowles standoff. These two ABC stars co-anchored the event with the clashing sensibilities of two women sharing the same man, or, in this case, rival super anchors sharing the same stage.

The British public has softened on Ms. Parker Bowles, Prince Charles's former mistress, who is now the Duchess of Cornwall and his second wife. On ABC the body language seemed stiffer.

"It is so great to spend this morning with you," Ms. Sawyer gushed to Ms. Walters.

"Glad we're doing it together," Ms. Walters said, more brusquely, before shifting to a solo. "This is the third royal wedding that I have covered, but I think this is the happiest."

The BBC didn't presume to look into the hearts of the royal couple. Mostly, Mr. Edwards and his colleagues provided historical background in the sotto voce of commentators at a golf tournament. They didn't get very excited about the bridal gown or the hats, though the eminent historian Simon Schama did have thoughts on the wedding décor.

"Those trees in the abbey are of course an echo of gothic vaulting," Mr. Schama said, noting that they brought to Westminster Abbey "a fresh note of dazzling springtime." (Mr. Schama as a wedding commentator is a bit like William F. Buckley covering the red carpet on Oscar night.)

Americans tended to look past the pageantry, tradition and protocol for signs of the newlyweds' true love — and other differences between this wedding and the other one. On Fox News, Joan Lunden said she was struck by "watching William come in with his brother, casually walking over to the crowd and kissing people, saying hello." Ms. Lunden, who covered Princess Diana's wedding for ABC News, added: "You had none of that in 1981 with Charles as he came in. It was much more formal." And a lot of the commentary was less formal, as well, even after the royals began entering Westminster Abbey. Ms. Couric described the Middletons' relationship with Queen Elizabeth and Prince Philip as "something out of 'Meet the Fockers.' "

Insouciance can go too far, however. Ms. Couric, speaking off the cuff, reported that the stout, bald man walking into the abbey with a cane was Mohamed al-Fayed, noting that it was "pretty shocking" that Mr. Fayed, the father of Dodi Fayed, Princess Diana's lover, who died at her side in the 1997 car accident, was invited. And it would have been, because Mr. Fayed has long accused the royal family of plotting to assassinate his son and Princess Diana. Actually, it was someone who looked like Mr. Fayed. CBS corrected the mistake later.

Most anchors adhered tightly to a script that called for royal harmony and a happier-ever-after ending. On ABC, Tina Brown, who wrote a biography of Princess Diana, couldn't stop praising the bride's "queenly" poise and aptitude for her new job.

"She's got the Windsor polish, it's all there," Ms. Brown said. "She's as regal as you can get and she's new to this whole way of life."

British Monarchy Scraps Rule of Male Succession in New Step to Modernization

BY JOHN F. BURNS | OCT. 28, 2011

LONDON — The 16 countries that recognize the British monarch as head of state struck a historic blow for women's rights on Friday, abolishing male precedence in the order of succession to the throne. But the possibility of a Catholic monarch will have to wait, nearly 500 years after Henry VIII broke with Rome.

The decision to overturn the centuries-old tradition known as primogeniture was accompanied by the scrapping of a constitutional prohibition on the monarch's marrying a Roman Catholic. But the rule that reserves the throne to Protestants will remain.

The changes will have no immediate impact on the existing line of succession. The current heir to the throne, Prince Charles, will retain that position, and is in any case the oldest child of his parents, Queen Elizabeth II and Prince Philip. The second in line to the throne is his firstborn child, Prince William. The new succession rule will come into play with William's children.

Indeed, it was the marriage last spring of Prince William and Kate Middleton, now the Duke and Duchess of Cambridge, that accelerated the change. Their wedding spurred a widespread sense that the young couple, by bringing a more contemporary influence to the royal court, are likely to have a far-reaching, if not determinate, impact on the monarchy's future.

With the change in the succession rules, their first child, if a girl, would automatically enter the line of succession as a future queen, instead of being relegated behind a younger brother as would have occurred under the rules that will now be abandoned.

"Put simply, if the Duke and Duchess of Cambridge were to have a little girl, that girl would one day be our queen," Prime Minister David

Cameron of Britain said in Perth, the city in western Australia where Commonwealth heads of government are holding a summit meeting

While the Cameron government took the lead in pushing the changes, it had to secure unanimous consent from the other countries that recognize the monarch as their head of state, a subset of the 54 countries that are members of the Commonwealth.

These include the nations of the so-called old Commonwealth, like Australia, Canada and New Zealand, and other countries that have gained their independence from Britain in recent decades. Those include the Bahamas, Jamaica and other Caribbean nations; Belize, in Central America; and three Pacific nations, Papua New Guinea, the Solomon Islands and Tuvalu.

The change comes at another important juncture in the modern monarchy, the 60th anniversary in February of the succession of Queen Elizabeth II to the throne.

The queen, now 85, has presided over a variety of changes in the monarchy over the past 30 years, agreeing to a gradual modernization that has swept away some of the stuffiness that critics have identified in an institution with origins going back at least 1,000 years.

After a series of unsuccessful attempts in Britain's Parliament to change the succession rules in recent years, the Cameron government, in office 18 months, put its weight fully behind the changes, and court officials said Queen Elizabeth was strongly supportive. Nearing the end of a 10-day trip to Australia that has drawn large crowds, she was in Perth in her capacity as head of the Commonwealth when the announcement was made.

The bar on the monarch's marrying a Catholic, like the rule on primogeniture, was enshrined in an array of statutes, most significantly in the Bill of Rights of 1689 and the Act of Settlement of 1701, which followed the turmoil of the monarchy of King James II, the last Catholic monarch.

The rules governing the monarchy were set after the violent upheavals that Britain endured in the 16th and 17th centuries after Henry VIII broke with Rome over control of the church in England, an event that led to centuries of marginalization, and often persecution, for Roman Catholics in Britain.

Over the centuries, legal discrimination against Catholics has been dismantled one brick at a time. Laws that forbade Catholics to serve in the army, own or inherit land, vote, hold public office or join one of the "learned professions" have been scrapped, leaving the provision forbidding the monarch to marry a Catholic exposed, as most Catholics have seen it, as a relic of the past.

The prohibition has seemed all the more incongruous for the fact that there is no similar bar on the monarch's marrying somebody from others faiths, including a Hindu, a Jew or a Muslim.

What remains unchanged in the succession rules is the requirement that the monarch be a Protestant, not a "Papist" as the Act of Settlement provided, and "in communion" with the Church of England.

That, in turn, is linked to the constitutional position of the Church of England as the country's established church, headed by the monarch. The Anglican primacy has come under a growing challenge by Britain's rapidly increasing ethnic and religious diversity in recent decades, particularly among Muslim leaders.

In his remarks in Perth, Mr. Cameron reaffirmed the rule that reserves the throne to a Protestant.

"Let me be clear," he said, "the monarch must be in communion with the Church of England, because he or she is the head of the church." He added, "But it is simply wrong to say they should be denied the right to marry a Catholic should they wish to do so."

Some experts said the change could lead to constitutional problems if a future monarch married a Catholic and the couple decided to bring up their children as Catholics, something the Vatican encourages.

But Archbishop Vincent Nichols, the head of the Catholic Church in England and Wales, told the BBC that the Catholic hierarchy would not precipitate a crisis over the issue.

"It's not unreasonable for the head of the Church of England to be an Anglican," he said.

A Royal Christening in Britain Amid a Refrain of Coos

BY KATRIN BENNHOLD | OCT. 23, 2013

LONDON — Some spent the night in the English rain, huddling under tarpaulins and keeping warm with flasks of tea outside St. James's Palace. It was all to secure a good view of Prince George of Cambridge on his christening day Wednesday. The prince had not been seen in public since he was born three months ago.

Apparently it was worth it. "Aww," the crowd cooed when the prince, third in line to the throne, arrived with his parents, Prince William and the Duchess of Cambridge, the former Kate Middleton. The sun was out and the prince was dressed in a lace and satin replica of the christening gown made for the eldest daughter of Queen Victoria in 1841. A royal christening has perhaps a special significance in a country that has its own church. Ever since Henry VIII broke with the Roman Catholic Church and established a more accommodating version in 1534 so he could divorce and re-wed (several times), Britain's royals have been the guardians of the Church of England. Prince George, in other words, will not just be king one day, he will be defender of the faith and supreme governor of the Church of England.

The archbishop of Canterbury, the Most Rev. Justin Welby, baptized the prince, whose full name is George Alexander Louis, with water from the River Jordan in a 45-minute ceremony. Archbishop Welby said he hoped that the event would inspire more Britons to come back to church.

If tradition was on ample display in some ways, in others it was conspicuously absent.

William and Kate, as the prince's popular parents are most commonly referred to here, did not pick the usual crop of senior or foreign royalty as godparents for their firstborn. They instead chose contemporaries, including childhood and university friends and a treasured palace employee.

Prince George of Cambridge was dressed in an intricate lace and satin replica of the christening gown made for the eldest daughter of Queen Victoria in 1841.

"It will be a long time before he is king — he might be a grandfather — and they want to have godparents that will follow him throughout his life," said Clarissa Campbell Orr, who specializes in the history of the monarchy at Anglia Ruskin University.

A celebrity photographer, Jason Bell, best-known for snapping Scarlett Johansson and David Beckham, was chosen to immortalize the event. Mr. Bell will take a much-awaited photo of Queen Elizabeth II with three future kings: Prince Charles, Prince William and Prince George — the first time four generations of the English royal succession will appear in a photograph together in more than a century.

Throughout the day, the memory of Prince William's mother, Diana, Princess of Wales, loomed large. Royal baptisms usually take place in the Music Room at Buckingham Palace, but the Chapel Royal in St. James's Palace was where Prince William, then 15, paid his respects at his mother's coffin before her funeral in 1997. Diana's close friend Julia Samuel was named one of the seven godparents. Later, at a private tea, guests were served christening cake, which per tradition was a tier from the couple's wedding cake.

As for Prince George, he looked peaceful, docile even, which must have been a relief for his father, who says he has "a voice to match any lion's roar."

Kate, Duchess of Cambridge, Gives Birth to Baby Girl

BY STEVEN ERLANGER | MAY 2, 2015

LONDON — Lo, and it came to pass at last on Saturday morning, unto Kate, who was late, a child was born — a baby girl, who will be fourth in line to the British throne.

There was much rejoicing in the land, especially among the many who had placed their bets on her having a girl, while others await a further windfall, if they guess right on what name will be chosen.

Kate, the Duchess of Cambridge, "was safely delivered of a daughter" at 8:34 a.m. London time, Kensington Palace announced. The birth came less than three hours after she was admitted to the hospital where in July 2013 she gave birth to Prince George, so according to the British media, she will get a 10 percent "loyalty discount" for her expensive hospital suite.

The baby weighs 8 pounds 3 ounces, the palace said, adding that mother and daughter were both doing well, and that father William, the Duke of Cambridge, was present for the birth of the child, who will be known as the Princess of Cambridge.

Prince Charles, the heir to the throne, had made it clear he was hoping for a granddaughter, and the child is the fifth great-grandchild of Queen Elizabeth II. The statement said senior royals had been informed and were "delighted with the news."

The impending birth has been a boon for Britain's bookmakers, who say they received thousands of bets on the newborn's gender and possible name. Even after Saturday's announcement, bets were still being placed on a name and other characteristics.

Alice and Charlotte are the clear favorites, followed by Elizabeth, Victoria and Diana — all names with royal heritage.

In 2013, the announcement of George's name came two days after his birth.

According to Ladbrokes, a bookmaker, bookies have paid out £250,000, or about $380,000, on the baby's gender. But they are also busy with bets on Thursday's British elections, among the tightest in memory. The birth is likely to draw attention away from the politicians, which may come as a relief in what has been a long campaign.

Kate, 33, who wed William, 32, in April 2011, had an April delivery date, she told friends. Royal watchers, fans and television camera operators have been lined up for days outside the Lindo wing at St. Mary's Hospital.

Prince William and Kate Try to Seem Normal

BY VANESSA FRIEDMAN | DEC. 10, 2014

SO WAS IT amazing, trendsetting, hemline-changing? Will it transform forever the fortunes of an obscure but hugely talented young designer, or alter the item on the top of everyone's Christmas wish list? Did, in other words, the visit of Prince William and Catherine, Duchess of Cambridge, a.k.a. Kate Middleton, to the East Coast this week have a fashion impact felt round the world?

Nah. It was more like a fashion flurry: Now you see it, now it evaporates from memory.

But while it may seem paradoxical, the Windsors' clothes, in their absolute boringness, made a serious statement.

NEILSON BARNARD/GETTY IMAGES

Prince William, Duke of Cambridge, and his wife, Catherine, Duchess of Cambridge, arriving at the Metropolitan Museum of Art for a fund-raiser for their alma mater, St. Andrews in Scotland.

In 1985, four years into their marriage, Diana, Princess of Wales, and her then-husband, Prince Charles, swept America off its feet during their Washington-Florida jaunt. This week, three years into their marriage, their son and his wife did the same. But where once all was fairy tale and filigree, this time it was more "Real Royals of Kensington Palace."

They fly commercial! They go to basketball games! And they wear the same things as you and me. The script was written in their style — especially so in the case of the five-months-pregnant Duchess of Cambridge. It makes some sense: She did not have any speeches scheduled, so her clothes spoke for her. At least in public.

From her first appearance on the way to the Carlyle hotel in New York in a burgundy tweed coat to the petrol silk gown she wore to the St. Andrews charity gala at the Metropolitan Museum of Art, Catherine displayed an image of extreme accessibility: aesthetically, financially and politically. (As did, to be fair, her husband — though social media and the paparazzi did not seem all that interested in his wardrobe choices, comparably speaking.) A recent move toward edgier styles, as demonstrated by the high-low hemline she wore to a National History Museum gala in London in October, was nowhere in evidence. Challenge was not on the agenda; outreach was.

Consider the list of brands, which included only one maternity label, Séraphine (bouclé coat, Day 1; black turtleneck dress, Day 3), as well as Goat (the black 1960s coat worn on Day 2), Beulah London (the lace cocktail dress, Day 1), Mulberry (pink coat, Day 3), Jenny Packham (gown, Day 3). If not exactly Main Street, the brands largely capped off before the top end. Especially because the obvious exception — the final evening gown for the Met gala — was actually a rare example of a royal shopping her closet: the Duchess of Cambridge had worn the dress twice before, including in 2013 to a 100 Women in Hedge Funds gala.

Then consider the looks: covered-up, knee-length, small-shouldered, round-necked, largely muted, awfully polite. Even the black lace cocktail dress the duchess wore to a private dinner for hedge fund managers flashed but a bit of arm, and called to mind only adjectives such as "appropriate" and "neat." When there was sparkle — a bit of Lurex here, some metallic there — it was discreetly done.

More interesting, then, was what the clothes did not represent.

They did not represent, for example, a real effort to "give British couturiers a huge boost" (a prediction of The Daily Mail) in the way that first ladies like Michelle Obama and Samantha Cameron have increasingly used their public profiles as tools to raise the global recognition of local designers. Rather, the effect was more a nod to small business than a major promotional push. The clothes were too forgettable, or familiar, for that.

Nor did they represent an effort to employ sartorial diplomacy, with Catherine embracing American names to demonstrate a form of aesthetic outreach.

Though she did make a gesture to local designers — wearing a Tory Burch silver tweed coat to watch an N.B.A. game at the Barclays Center in Brooklyn along with J. Crew stretch jeans, and sporting Stuart Weitzman black court pumps and a Muse bag throughout her visit — it wasn't prolonged enough to make a real point. As a result, the choices seemed less about strategic trans-Atlantic boosterism and more about the youthful midmarket: coat price, $595; jeans, currently on sale for $105; pumps, $355, amortized over the visit. As for the bag, she has been, well, clutching it in various colors since 2012.

And they did not even seem like an effort to make a point about the dos and don'ts of contemporary pregnancy dress, as the coat parade largely obviated the whole burgeoning stomach issue.

CHAPTER 3

Prince Harry and Meghan Markle

For some, the engagement of Prince Harry to Meghan Markle, an American actress with African-American ancestry, came as a sign of hope for race and immigration relations in the United Kingdom's future. However, others cautioned against pointing to the engagement as a sign of real change, instead calling it merely symbolic. Media coverage of Prince Harry prior to his engagement portrays him as human. His relatability coupled with Meghan Markle's presence in the public eye may usher in an age of transparency among the royals.

For Prince Harry, Vegas Exploits Didn't Stay There

BY JOHN F. BURNS | AUG. 23, 2012

LONDON — A year that has featured a triumphant Olympic Games and Queen Elizabeth II's Diamond Jubilee struck an unwelcome bump on Wednesday for the royal family with the publication of photographs showing the queen's sometimes wayward grandson, Prince Harry, naked and cavorting with a naked woman, or women, during a strip billiards game in a Las Vegas hotel room.The photographs, on a Hollywood celebrity Web site, TMZ, were confirmed as genuine on Wednesday by aghast palace officials in London. The 27-year-old prince, whose boisterous ways are said to have alternately amused and infuriated his 86-year-old grandmother in the past, was reported to have flown back to London on Wednesday afternoon in a subdued mood, certain to face a family rebuke for slipping back into unprincely ways.

The incident was all the more jarring in a year that had otherwise gone so well for the royals. Crowds for the monarch's 60th anniversary on the throne have been large, and jubilant. The queen's popularity jumped when she played herself in the paradiving-with-James-Bond spoof that was part of the widely praised Olympics opening ceremony. Her granddaughter Zara Phillips, Harry's cousin, won a silver medal as an equestrian.

Harry, son of Princess Diana and third in line to the British throne after Prince Charles and Prince William, mingled with athletes at the Olympics almost every day and represented the queen in the V.I.P. enclosure at the closing ceremony. He drew fulsome comments from British columnists, who said he appeared to have matured beyond his "wild days," when he was regularly photographed in British newspapers tumbling, often visibly intoxicated, out of London's priciest nightclubs.

In Las Vegas, he was taking what palace aides described as a brief, post-Olympics break before preparing to resume his duties as a pilot of an Apache attack helicopter, with the army rank of captain. Army officials have said that he has trained for combat duties in Afghanistan, and may be deployed there in the fall.

The prince's American trip made the front pages in Britain with photographs of the bachelor Harry kibitzing poolside with young women in bikinis. But then came the photographs of Harry, naked, with an equally naked woman — or women.

The photographs were confirmed as genuine on Wednesday by St. James's Palace. The BBC reported late on Wednesday that royal aides had asked Britain's newspaper watchdog, the Press Complaints Commission, to warn British newspapers not to publish them. But The Sun, a Rupert Murdoch tabloid, published one of the photographs on the front page of its Thursday editions.

Both photographs on TMZ were blurry and awkwardly framed, as if taken surreptitiously with a cellphone camera. One showed a naked

Harry, side-face to the camera with his hands over his abdomen, with what appeared to be a naked woman close behind him. The other showed Harry, again naked, facing away from the camera, grasping a woman who appears to be naked from behind. Beside them was a pool table.

An accompanying article on TMZ said the photographs were taken on Friday night in the prince's "V.I.P. suite" at the Wynn hotel, where accommodations can run up to $1,500 a night. It said it did not know who the women were, and it offered no information about how the photographs had come to be taken, or how TMZ had obtained them.

The article said Harry left Las Vegas for London after the photographs were posted on Tuesday, and did not mingle with other passengers. "He stayed in the upstairs cabin of the 747," it said.

Reaction in Britain ran the gamut from dismay to loyalist defense of the prince and, more commonly, to amusement. The BBC reported that palace officials were suffering from "acute embarrassment."

Among people surveyed at random in central London, including subway commuters reading about the Las Vegas incident on the front page of the tabloid the Evening Standard, the verdict was mostly thumbs-up.

"I think it's quite funny," said John Daniels, 46, a hedge fund manager. "I'm sure most people would like to be doing exactly the same thing, especially in Vegas. This is his own private time and people shouldn't be taking photographs of him."

Gordon Fleming, 79, a retired civil engineer from Scotland, said: "He should be able to enjoy himself. If I was still a young man, I'd be doing it, too."

SANDY MACASKILL CONTRIBUTED REPORTING.

Who Wants to Be King?
No One, Prince Harry Says

BY CHRISTINE HAUSER | JUNE 22, 2017

PRINCE HARRY, who is fifth in line to the British throne, has said that he does not think anyone in the royal family wants to be king or queen, but that the family of Queen Elizabeth II will carry on the succession out of a sense of duty.

"We're involved in modernizing the British monarchy," the prince, 32, told Newsweek in an interview published online on Wednesday.

"We are not doing this for ourselves but for the greater good of the people," he said. "Is there any one of the royal family who wants to be king or queen? I don't think so, but we will carry out our duties at the right time."

The prince also said that his personal priority was to lead an "ordinary" life. He credited his mother, Princess Diana, who died in a car crash in Paris in 1997, with inspiring him to do so.

"My mother took a huge part in showing me an ordinary life, including taking me and my brother to see homeless people," Prince Harry was quoted as saying, referring to his elder brother, Prince William. "Thank goodness I'm not completely cut off from reality. People would be amazed by the ordinary life William and I live."

"I do my own shopping. Sometimes, when I come away from the meat counter in my local supermarket, I worry someone will snap me with their phone," he added. "But I am determined to have a relatively normal life, and if I am lucky enough to have children, they can have one too. Even if I was king, I would do my own shopping."

Asked if he thought too much "ordinary" might make the royal family too accessible and take away its mystery, the prince said: "It's a tricky balancing act. We don't want to dilute the magic."

"The British public and the whole world need institutions like it," he said.

The interview took place at the prince's two-bedroom cottage at Kensington Palace in London. The report included anecdotes from the prince's official appearances over the past year, where it said members of the public were "thrilled to be talking to, as one said, 'an actual prince.' "

In the line of succession, Prince Harry comes after his father, Prince Charles; Prince William; and Prince William's children, Prince George and Princess Charlotte.

His remarks were his latest to indicate a shift within the British monarchy toward greater openness, led by a younger generation. In a podcast released in April, Prince Harry shared rare details of the private life of a member of the royal family when he spoke of suffering emotionally for years after the death of his mother before finally getting help.

In the Newsweek interview, he again brought up the impact that her death had on him, particularly as a 12-year-old child who walked in his mother's funeral procession with the eyes of the entire world on him.

"My mother had just died, and I had to walk a long way behind her coffin, surrounded by thousands of people watching me while millions more did on television," he told the magazine.

"I don't think any child should be asked to do that, under any circumstances," he said. "I don't think it would happen today."

He has also denounced, in an unusual statement issued through his spokesman last November, the "racial undertones" of British news coverage and social media harassment of his new girlfriend, the American actress Meghan Markle, whose mother is black and whose father is white.

On June 15, Prince Harry, who told Newsweek that he often wanted to be "something other than Prince Harry," rolled up his sleeves, sampled food from carts and chatted with people during an official appearance at Borough Market near the Thames, less than two weeks after terrorists went on a stabbing rampage there.

The monarchy and the costs used to support it have often been the subject of scrutiny, such as last November when a decision to renovate Buckingham Palace at a cost of £369 million (about $456 million) came amid years of national budget cuts.

Prince Harry's remarks in Newsweek renewed discussion on social media about whether the monarchy was outdated.

"Prince Harry wants us to see him as an ordinary chap, who does his own shopping — but he is not," wrote James Moore, a columnist, in the Independent. "It is true that he was exposed to the darker side of life in Britain while growing up, but he will never know the feeling of wondering whether he has enough money to pay for that shopping at the till.

"That said, a gilded cage is still a cage, and escape is next to impossible," he wrote.

Prince Harry, Almost Just Like Us

BY GUY TREBAY | MAY 17, 2013

GREENWICH, CONN. — "It's ballet at speed," Malcolm Borwick, captain of the Sentebale team, said Wednesday morning, referring to polo, the so-called sport of kings. Like many top athletes in the sport, Mr. Borwick follows a peripatetic international circuit, playing 110 games a year that take him from Florida to the Gulf States to Brazil.

Most prominent among his three teammates on Wednesday, the man who had drawn the satellite trucks and the camera crews and 200 members of the international press and another couple of hundred paying guests to the Greenwich Polo Club on a cold and rainy Wednesday morning was, of course, Prince Harry, the ginger-haired rake who currently stands third in line of succession to the British throne.

"If you're super optimistic, and very positive, as Harry is," you'll be effective on the field, suggested Mr. Borwick, a six-goal player. As it happened, the prince's optimism, if that's what it was, carried the Sentebale team, named for the charity he sponsors in the African nation of Lesotho, to success.

As polo goes, it was a middling game, notable for some strategic defensive plays by Dawn Jones, the sole woman player; some spirited runs by Nacho Figueras, the Argentine heartthrob (and six-goal player) and Ralph Lauren model; and for the reality that nobody in the stands paid the slightest attention to the doings of anybody but the English prince.

"It must be so hard, being Prince Harry all the time," said the Canadian model Jessica Stam, who despite the suburban setting and soggy weather, was dressed in a severe structured black dress by Thom Browne and a pair of that designer's stiletto wing tips. "Everything is Prince Harry, Prince Harry, Prince Harry," she added. Wouldn't it be nice, she said, to be just plain Harry every once in a while?

FRED R. CONRAD/THE NEW YORK TIMES

Prince Harry playing in the Sentebale Polo Cup exhibition match in Greenwich, Conn. The event drew a couple of hundred guests, including a few celebrities and models, and a similarly large number of media people.

File under: "Never Going to Happen." True, the prince has made some admirable attempts to escape the stultifying formality of his role and position. There was the notorious 2012 strip billiards game in a Las Vegas V.I.P. suite, for instance, a public relations debacle the memory of which his brief recent tour of the United States was intended to erase. While arguably, in the age of smartphones, the prince's night in Vegas showed little evidence of a sharp and calculating intelligence, it probably did an awful lot to raise his Klout ratings, which is never a bad thing. Google "naked prince" and see what that gets you.

Next try ribbon-cutting prince.

That it was not the ribbon cutter people came out for on Wednesday could be judged from the swooning crowd of women in elaborate hats and fawning men in pastel cashmere sweaters and spectator shoes and also the highly attentive designer Valentino Garavani, who arrived with Giancarlo Giammetti, his business partner — both in down puffers and with meticulous coiffures, their skin tanned a hue reminiscent of the ribs special at Dallas BBQ.

The 28-year-old prince appeared after guests had been seated for a tented lunch whose sponsors included Royal Salute whisky, Range Rover and Garrard jewelers, and delivered a short speech about his charity. As his mother once had, he spoke with feeling about the effects of H.I.V. and AIDS on children in sub-Saharan Africa ("It is dangerous to have it and even more dangerous not to talk about it," the prince said) and then sat to a meal of beef tenderloin, a salad of mesclun with peas and baby carrots, and the rapt attention of every single human in the room.

"He's really normal," Karolina Kurkova, the model and the prince's right-hand neighbor at lunch (Stephanie Seymour was at his left), said after the meal ended. By that time many of the more forward guests — the television personality Gayle King was one, Mr. Garavani was another — managed to defy security injunctions against approaching the presence to barge up to the table and bend the prince's ear.

"It can't be easy," achieving normalcy, said Avril Graham, executive fashion and beauty editor at Harper's Bazaar, adding that in the life of the royals, "You're shunted from place to place, and everything is shined up and repainted. And we all know what it's like to be with people who are used to having things done for them."

We do. They are spoiled and pettish and imperious and regal and in general in no apparent way like the British prince, who conducted himself in such a low-key fashion that he did seem sort of normal, or as normal as anyone can be whose grandmother is Queen Elizabeth II.

"What do you think my chances are with Harry?" a young socialite wrote on the back of her place card, slipping it to a friend across the table. Though the reply was positive, the logistics were likely to prove a challenge: the young prince was leaving for England right after the game.

"Do you think," the young woman added in a postscript, that a mutual friend might "diss him because he's a ginger?"

At a guess, this reporter thought not.

Prince Harry, in His Mother's Footsteps

BY RALPH BLUMENTHAL | MAY 29, 2009

IT WASN'T EXACTLY what the British press had flown 3,500 miles to see: Prince Harry upstaged by a tree.

But there was the seething mass of news people penned behind police barricades, there was the tree — a Magnolia "Elizabeth," just planted in a downtown Manhattan memorial garden — and there was His Royal Highness, Princess Diana's younger son, third in line to the throne and a veteran of the Afghanistan war, shoveling soil, half-hidden behind the leaves.

"Harry, we can't see you!" voices brayed. "Come around front!"

The young prince obliged, happy no doubt to be making the kind of news that would not leave his family cringing.

Twenty years and four months after his mother enraptured New York with her own royal visit, Prince Harry, 24, arrived in a city fought over by his forebears, with a ginger toe-dipping in the waters of international relations, centering on acts of charity and a commemoration of the Sept. 11 attacks. It was a somber visit clearly designed to temper the prince's tabloid reputation as a hearty partier with a penchant for gaffes, like making derogatory videos and wearing Nazi regalia to a costume party. Flag-waving crowds lined up to cheer him, with adoring young women particularly plentiful. One was Roseanne Krylowski, 25, a Rutgers University student, who waited in the financial district with a sign that said "NYC ♥ Prince Harry."

"I'm hoping to have a detailed conversation that ends with him asking for a date," she said.

Within hours of arriving from London on Friday on a commercial ticket that was privately paid for by his grandmother, Queen Elizabeth, the strawberry blond prince, in a dark blue suit, blue-and-white striped shirt and the maroon-and-blue striped regimental tie of the Household Division, laid a wreath at the site of the World Trade Center.

Prince Harry planted a tree at the British Garden at Hanover Square, which memorializes Britons killed in the attack on the World Trade Center.

He spoke to firefighters and relatives of 9/11 victims and looked over blueprints for the site's reconstruction. "Big question," he asked at one point. "When is this supposed to be finished?"

Then he dedicated the British Garden at Hanover Square, between Stone and Pearl Streets, which is a memorial to the 67 British people killed at the trade center. He planted the magnolia there and attended a private meeting with victims' families.

The garden, paved in Scottish stone with markings to evoke the British Isles, is under the patronage of his father, Prince Charles, who visited in 2005. "So you'll be able to tell him the progress," said Camilla Hellman, president of the garden trust.

"Very, very well done," said Harry, who spoke sparingly.

In the afternoon, accompanied by a British soldier, Joe Townsend, 21, who lost his legs in Afghanistan, Prince Harry, who is training to be a helicopter pilot like his elder brother, William, toured the Veterans Affairs Hospital on East 23rd Street.

He visited a prosthetics section, shaking the artificial hand of a gulf war veteran, Paul Yarbrough, and jokingly wincing at the strong grip: "Owww!"

He met behind closed doors with other wounded veterans, and afterward, John Loosen, the chief of prosthetics, said the prince spoke of their camaraderie. "He commented on how he felt people who didn't do what they did don't understand," he said.

On Saturday morning, Harry is scheduled to visit the Harlem Children's Zone with Prince Seeiso of Lesotho, a kingdom-enclave within South Africa, who is his co-patron in a charity called Sentebale.

And in the afternoon, the prince, an accomplished polo player, is to take part in a match on Governors Island sponsored by Veuve Clicquot, the Champagne label, with proceeds going to American Friends of Sentebale.

He plans to leave for home right after the match. The schedule left little time for personal amusement — which seemed to be the point.

Peter Brown, a British publicist in New York who once ran the Beatles' management company and advised the Consulate on Princess Diana's visit in February 1989, said it all sounded familiar. When he was helping to plan Harry's mother's trip, the directive was clear: "She must at no time look like she was enjoying herself."

Diana managed to enthrall anyway, wowing an audience at the Brooklyn Academy of Music and attending a banquet at the World Financial Center. But she also toured the Henry Street Settlement on the Lower East Side and cuddled children with AIDS — pointedly without donning gloves — in the pediatric unit at Harlem Hospital Center.

Her second son, who was 4 at the time of his mother's visit, won high marks from some for his performance on Friday. "It's easy to be rude to the royal family but they've been hugely supportive," said Alex Clarke of London, who lost her 30-year-old daughter, Suria, an employee of Cantor Fitzgerald, in the trade center attack.

Suffering a twinge of disappointment was Ms. Krylowski, the Rutgers student, who was standing behind a barricade that Harry did not stop at. "I won't be a princess after all," she said.

Also keeping hope alive for some more reportable news were members of the British press.

"He's got 24 hours to go," said Jonathan Hunt, a British journalist at the Fox News Channel in New York. "He could still do anything."

Prince Harry Denounces Media Coverage of His Girlfriend, Meghan Markle

BY STEVEN ERLANGER | NOV. 8, 2016

LONDON — Prince Harry on Tuesday attacked the "racial undertones" of British news coverage and social media harassment of his new girlfriend, the American actress Meghan Markle.

In an unusual statement, the prince, the 32-year-old grandson of Queen Elizabeth II, said that a line had been crossed in the reporting of his relationship with Ms. Markle, 35, whose mother is black and whose father is white.

"Some of this has been very public," read the statement, issued in the name of the prince's spokesman, Jason Knauf. "The smear on the front page of a national newspaper; the racial undertones of comment pieces; and the outright sexism and racism of social media trolls and web article comments."

The role and behavior of the news media are a particularly sensitive topic for Prince Harry and his brother, Prince William. Their mother, Diana, died in Paris in a 1997 car crash when pursued by paparazzi.

Both princes, who were then 12 and 15, have said that their mother's death made them wary of the news media, though the royal family has generally been skillful in getting favorable coverage and suppressing scandal.

But internet competition and social media activity have accelerated and coarsened coverage of the prince's relationship with a divorced, biracial woman who was already in the public eye as an actress.

Since articles surfaced about Ms. Markle's dating Prince Harry, the British tabloids have expressed surprise that a "brunette" would be his type and accused her of not being British enough for him.

The Daily Mail ran an article headlined, "Harry's girl is (almost) straight outta Compton: Gang-scarred home of her mother revealed — so will he be dropping by for tea?"

The article then wove together various racial stereotypes, lamenting Ms. Markle's mother's "gang-scarred" Los Angeles neighborhood, Crenshaw, and its "tatty one-story homes," and listing crime statistics for the area.

Newspapers have been digging up suggestive photographs of Ms. Markle and examining her past relationships, and some comments on their websites and on social media have been explicit and racist.

The prince's statement, which confirmed his long-rumored relationship with Ms. Markle, expressed fears for her safety and privacy. It noted that his office had regularly fought to keep defamatory articles out of the newspapers — which he said had offered large bribes to her ex-boyfriend.

The statement also condemned the way that the news media has invaded Ms. Markle's privacy and harassed her mother.

In one instance, a palace official said a photographer had chased an assistant to Ms. Markle through the garage of her home in Toronto. The photographer had to be physically removed and the police called, the official said.

One article in the tabloid The Sun was about Ms. Markle's appearing on Pornhub, an adult website, even though the "steamy scenes," as the newspaper called them, were not pornography but taken from a television series she acts in, "Suits."

The Sun also ran a headline above an interview with Ms. Markle's estranged sister, saying, "Don't fall for my little sis, Harry, she'd be the next Princess Pushy," a reference to the unkind nickname for Princess Michael of Kent.

One comment piece in last weekend's Mail on Sunday, by Rachel Johnson, said of Ms. Markle: "Genetically, she is blessed. If there is issue from her alleged union with Prince Harry, the Windsors will thicken their watery, thin blue blood and Spencer pale skin and ginger hair with some rich and exotic DNA."

Ms. Markle described herself as biracial in an August 2015 interview with Elle magazine, saying, "My dad is Caucasian and my mom is African-American. I'm half black and half white." The essay also discussed some of the racism she has experienced as a result.

Afua Hirsch, writing in The Guardian, said: "It's a subtle point, easily missed. Meghan Markle, Prince Harry's apparent new love, is a 'glamorous brunette,' 'a departure from Prince Harry's usual type' and 'not in the society blonde style of previous girlfriends,' according to The Daily Mail. I think what they are trying to say is that Markle, actor, global development ambassador and lifestyle blogger, is black."

Even more scandalous to the tabloids, wrote Ms. Hirsch, is that Ms. Markle is older and divorced and played somewhat "raunchy scenes" in "Suits" and that "her mother is visibly black, with dreadlocks."

Ms. Markle, who graduated from Northwestern University in 2003, married in 2011 and divorced two years later, a fact that has also been the source of attention from the news media.

Prince Harry has criticized the news media before, but never in such an angry and formal fashion. He has gotten into public trouble in the past, with leaked photographs of parties in Las Vegas or wearing a Nazi costume.

"Prince Harry is worried about Ms. Markle's safety and is deeply disappointed that he has not been able to protect her," the statement said. "It is not right that a few months into a relationship with him that Ms. Markle should be subjected to such a storm."

"He knows commentators will say this is 'the price she has to pay' and that 'this is all part of the game,' " the statement continued. "He strongly disagrees. This is not a game — it is her life and his."

Ms. Markle is best known for her role as Rachel Zane on the television legal drama "Suits," and she played an F.B.I. agent in the science-fiction series "Fringe."

She has also been involved in charitable work with nongovernmental organizations. Ms. Markle became a global ambassador for World Vision Canada this year, traveling to Rwanda for its clean water campaign, and she has worked for gender equality and women's empowerment.

Prince Harry, Meghan Markle and News of a Royal Wedding

BY KIMIKO DE FREYTAS-TAMURA | NOV. 27, 2017

LONDON — He is a flame-haired former wild child, who courted controversy in his youth by smoking cannabis and by once wearing a Nazi uniform to a party. She is a biracial, divorced actress from abroad. Together, they are taking the British monarchy — that most conservative of institutions — into a more modern era.

Prince Harry, a grandson of Queen Elizabeth II and fifth in line to the throne, is engaged to Meghan Markle, his American girlfriend, the royal family said on Monday.

The prince, 33, and Ms. Markle, 36, will marry in the spring, a statement from Clarence House added.

Prince Harry and Ms. Markle's engagement underscores recent shifts in the British monarchy. They are part of a new generation of royals eager to project themselves as modern, inclusive and down-to-earth. This latest set of royals, who include the duke and duchess of Cambridge — Prince Harry's elder brother, William, and his sister-in-law, Catherine — have in recent years tried to connect better with the public.

It is a marked difference, for example, from the queen, who has maintained a more traditionally aloof style.

Prince Harry and Ms. Markle are expected to be known as the duke and duchess of Sussex after they are married, according to the British news media, although she may be known informally as Princess Meghan. If Prince Harry were to decline the dukedom, he would remain Prince Henry of Wales — his official name.

The pair have dated for more than a year, and made their first official outing together in September in Toronto at the Invictus Games, a Paralympic-style competition for wounded or sick members of the military and veterans.

Prince Harry and Meghan Markle during an official photocall to announce their engagement at The Sunken Gardens at Kensington Palace on November 27, 2017 in London.

Like his brother, Prince Harry grew up in the public eye, first as a son of the heir to the throne, and then as an adolescent struggling over the loss of his mother, Princess Diana, who died in a car accident when he was 12. His grief played out in what he described as "total chaos" in his 20s, a period that was gleefully pounced on by the tabloids.

The relationship of Prince Harry and Ms. Markle also has been the subject of intense scrutiny.

The announcement of their engagement ended days of fevered speculation by the British news media, some of which, in anticipation of the event, tried to find any royal connection with Ms. Markle. (The Daily Telegraph breathlessly reported an unverified study showing that Ms. Markle's ancestor was an aristocrat who was beheaded by Henry VIII, a distant relative of Prince Harry.)

But other stories about Ms. Markle's ethnicity and middle-class background — her mother is a black yoga instructor and her father is a white cinematographer — have drawn the ire of the royal family. The prince himself issued an unusual statement last year, denouncing the "racial undertones" of news coverage of Ms. Markle.

Prince Harry's reputation has changed markedly in recent years. In his younger days, he acknowledged wanting to be a "bad boy," but he has emerged as possibly Britain's most popular royal.

As a rebellious youth, he partied heavily, including an episode in 2005, when he wore a Nazi costume with a swastika armband, just weeks before his grandmother, Queen Elizabeth, was scheduled to lead Holocaust memorial ceremonies.

In 2009, a video emerged of him using racial slurs during his first tour of duty in Afghanistan. In the footage, he is seen referring to a Pakistani member of his platoon as a "our little Paki friend" and calls another soldier a "raghead." He later apologized.

But he has matured since those early years, say his defenders, becoming a vocal advocate for mental health awareness and for other charities. He has also spoken openly about the difficulties he faced after the death of Princess Diana.

In another unusual break from palace protocol, he divulged to a newspaper that he had suffered for years from grief after the death of his mother, before finally getting help about three years ago at the urging of Prince William.

In 2016, he took an H.I.V. test and broadcast it live on the royals' Facebook page in 2016 to promote the importance being tested for the virus that causes AIDS.

This year, he suggested that no one in the royal family really wanted to sit on the throne. "We are involved in modernizing the British monarchy," he said in an interview with Newsweek. "We are not doing this for ourselves but for the greater good of the people.

Prince Harry's public statement last year in defense of Ms. Markle effectively confirmed their relationship, and it also took aim at the British newspapers that have long hungered for news of the royals and their foibles.

In the blunt rebuke, Prince Harry, through his spokesman, excoriated "the smear on the front page of a national newspaper; the racial undertones of comment pieces; and the outright sexism and racism of social media trolls and web article comments."

In their first interview since the announcement, Ms. Markle revealed that she had very little understanding of the British royal family and its significance.

"I didn't know much about him," she told the BBC, referring to her fiancé, adding that the pair had been set up on a blind date by a friend.

"The only thing I asked her was, 'Was he nice?' "

Prince Harry said he tried to prepare her for the media scrutiny. "I tried to warn you as much as possible," he said. Still, "we were totally surprised by the reaction. We were totally unprepared."

When asked about the way she has been portrayed by some British media, Ms. Markle replied: "It's a shame that that is the climate in this world. At the end of the day I'm proud of who I am and where I come from. We just focus on who we are as a couple."

Their relationship is not the first in which a British royal has fallen in love with an American partner who had been married before.

King Edward VIII caused a constitutional crisis in 1936 before he abdicated to marry the American socialite Wallis Simpson, who was divorced. The Church of England at the time opposed the marriage, and the king chose love over his royal duties, with his brother taking his place to become King George VI.

Harry's parents, Prince Charles and Princess Diana, divorced in 1996.

Prince Harry served on active duty in the British military for about a decade, rising to the rank of captain. He served two tours in Afghanistan, where he co-piloted an Apache helicopter and was a weapons officer.

The announcement of the engagement was quickly followed by messages of congratulations from the queen and her husband, Prince Philip, who recently celebrated 70 years of marriage. The couple said they were "delighted" and wished Prince Harry and Ms. Markle "every happiness."

Prince Charles, Harry's father, said he was "thrilled," while Prime Minister Theresa May said in a statement that the engagement marked "a time of huge celebration and excitement."

Prince William and Catherine, who is known as Kate, said they were "very excited for Harry and Meghan." The date of Prince Harry and Ms. Markle's wedding may take place close to another royal event, the birth of William and Kate's third child, due in April.

Kate's wedding to Prince William was also unusual in the context of the royal family because she was a commoner: Her parents had founded a mail-order party supply company.

Ms. Markle's parents, Doria Ragland and Thomas Markle, said they were "incredibly happy" for their daughter and her prince.

Ms. Markle describes herself as biracial. She graduated from Northwestern University in Illinois in 2003, and married in 2011, divorcing two years later.

She is best known for her roles in the television legal drama "Suits" and in the science-fiction series "Fringe," and she appeared on the cover of Vanity Fair in September. Ms. Markle is also notable for her charitable work — she is a global ambassador for World Vision Canada — and she has worked for gender equality and women's empowerment.

She also shares a love of dogs with the queen, who is known for having a collection of corgis. British tabloids reported this month that Ms. Markle was preparing to move her two dogs, Bogart, a Labrador-shepherd mix, and Guy, a beagle, to London.

ANNA SCHAVERIEN, SUSANNE FOWLER AND PRASHANT S. RAO CONTRIBUTED REPORTING.

The Prince and the Actress

OPINION | BY THE NEW YORK TIMES | NOV. 29, 2017

READER COMMENTS in Britain on the engagement of Prince Harry and Meghan Markle have an inevitable sprinkling of the enough-already-about-the-royal-family variety. But not many. Most reflect a genuine fascination, ranging from simple expressions of good wishes to commentaries on royal weddings past and the significance of a popular, modern prince marrying a mixed-race American actress.

There's a lot of grist there. And it couldn't come at a better time: Britain in the throes of a miserable divorce from the European Union; Europe (and America) dealing with nationalist and even racist sentiments; sex-pest revelations everywhere — a whole world, it seems, in desperate need of diversion and romance.

We have learned why Ms. Markle may soon be the duchess of Sussex but will never be "Princess Meg" ("princess" is reserved for royal blood) and has almost no chance of being queen (Prince Harry is now fifth in line for the throne, and when Catherine, duchess of Cambridge, to use Kate's formal name, has her child, he will drop to sixth).

This and much more we have discovered or rediscovered, all to the refrain of "how things have changed." A royal prince marrying an American whose mother is African-American, who is divorced to boot, is not something that could have happened 100 years ago, maybe not even 20. When the British tabloids first found out about the relationship a year ago and let loose, Prince Harry was compelled to issue a fierce broadside denouncing "racial undertones" in some of the commentaries.

Yet it is by breaking taboos that Britain's royal family has remained not only entertaining, but also relevant to all the many people who ardently follow them. Diana, Princess of Wales, remains revered as the "peoples' princess" for refusing to be constrained by barriers of tradition and snobbery, and her sons, Prince William, the heir apparent, and Prince Harry have been true to her legacy.

Prince Harry has become possibly the most popular of the royals by being arguably the most modern, in part through his history of questionable behavior, but also for his cheeky smile, distinguished military service and dedication to worthy causes like the Invictus Games, a sporting event for wounded or disabled veterans he created. It was at the Invictus event in Toronto in September that the English prince and the American actress of mixed race made their first public appearance, holding hands, laughing and even kissing.

The global fascination with British royals ensures a long and lively discussion of the engagement and what it means for British identity, royal lineage and whatnot. But Prince Harry and Ms. Markle have already given their simple and admirable answer, that their very public world is not one in which class, background, nationality or race are obstacles to love.

Prince Harry Used Princess Diana's Diamonds in Engagement Ring

BY NIRAJ CHOKSHI | NOV. 27, 2017

There was something old and something new in the ring Meghan Markle, the American actress, wore when she and Prince Harry announced their engagement on Monday.

The ring, which the prince himself designed, bore three glittering diamonds: a central stone from Botswana and two others from the collection of the prince's mother, Princess Diana, who died in 1997, the couple said in a joint interview shared on social media on Monday.

"It's incredibly special to be able to have this, which sort of links where you come from and Botswana, which is important to us, and it's perfect," Ms. Markle said to Prince Harry during the interview. The ring is yellow gold, Ms. Markle's favorite, Prince Harry said.

The couple dated for about a year and a half before becoming engaged this month. Just weeks into their relationship, Prince Harry invited Ms. Markle on a five-day trip to Botswana.

"Then we were really by ourselves, which was crucial to me," he said during the interview.

The prince, 33, and Ms. Markle, 36, appeared for photographers at Kensington Palace's Sunken Garden on Monday shortly after announcing the engagement.

The ring was made by Cleave and Company, official jewelers to Queen Elizabeth II. The company's director said in a statement that it was "greatly honored to have been of service."

The couple, who were introduced by a mutual friend, said in the interview that they knew little about each other before meeting. As an American, Ms. Markle said she wasn't very familiar with British royalty, and Prince Harry had never watched "Suits," the legal drama on which Ms. Markle portrays the character Rachel Zane.

Prince Harry and Ms. Markle, whose father is white and whose mother is black, had been subjected to intense and sometimes racially charged scrutiny by the British news media, which avidly covers the royal family.

"We were totally unprepared," Prince Harry said of the scrutiny they faced as a couple, noting that they had tried to steel themselves for what would come.

In an unusual statement last year, the prince accused the news media of crossing a line and said he was worried about Ms. Markle's safety. His mother, Diana, was killed in Paris two decades ago in a car crash while being pursued by paparazzi.

Prince Harry proposed at home one night this month as the couple prepared dinner together, they said in the interview.

"She didn't let me finish. She said: 'Can I say yes? Can I say yes?' " Prince Harry said. "Then there was hugs and I had the ring in my finger and I said, 'Can I give you the ring?' And she said, 'Oh, yes, the ring!' "

The wedding is planned for the spring.

Prince Harry Casts Aside Ghosts of Royal Marriages Past

BY SARAH LYALL | NOV. 27, 2017

ONCE UPON A TIME, in 1936, a British monarch named Edward VIII was forbidden to marry his divorced American girlfriend and also be king, so he renounced the throne, moved with her to France and lived not-so-happily ever after.

Nearly 20 years later, forced to make a similarly unpleasant choice, Edward's niece Margaret opted to keep her title but jettison her (also divorced) boyfriend. She ended up herself divorced from the man she married in the boyfriend's place.

But that was another century, another world and many divorces ago.

As we ponder the news that Prince Harry, the raffish younger son of the future king of England, has become engaged to Meghan Markle — an American actress who, like nearly everyone in this story so far (except Harry) is divorced — it is worth noting how dramatically Britain and the royal family have changed in the intervening years.

It is also worth noting that the engagement, announced in front of Kensington Palace with traditional fanfare, the unveiling of a massive diamond engagement ring and a burst of details about who-said-what-to-whom-when and how they knew that this was it, is at once a huge deal, and not much of one at all.

It is not a big deal because Prince Harry, 33, a former army officer with an earthy sense of humor who brings an element of edgy sex appeal to a family that could use a bit more of it, is only fifth in line to the throne. The only way he could plausibly become king is under some sort of "And Then There Were None" or "Kind Hearts and Coronets" scenario involving his grandmother, Queen Elizabeth; his father, Prince Charles; his brother, Prince William; and William's young children, George and Charlotte.

But the engagement is significant, in part as a frivolously welcome distraction at a time of unrelenting bad news about the economy, about Britain's painful "Brexit" from Europe and about Britain's place in the world. More than that, it is an example of openness and inclusivity in a country that is sorely divided over issues like race and immigration.

Ms. Markle's father is white and her mother is African-American, and so with one heady announcement, it seems, Harry and Ms. Markle have thrown out generations' worth of quietly repressed tradition and presented a new royal model to a country that will have to adjust to it, whether it wants to or not.

"The royal family and the standards they normally have — they want them to be white and not divorced," said Asha Duncan, 31, who works in fashion advertising and was strolling in Kensington on Monday. "Maybe she will get them moving with the times more," she said of Ms. Markle, "showing we live in a multicultural society."

Visiting from Boston, Trevor Gailun, who is 41 and works in finance, said the emergence of a royal American in London could be only a plus.

"It's very exciting that we have an American woman," he said. "I think it is good for the royal family and also for the world to have a little bit more diversity."

Not only that, he said, but "Americans are celebrity obsessed, and I think having a pretty well-known actress now as a princess — it does not really get better than that."

Everyone loves an engagement almost as much as they love a wedding, and Britain's monarchy-obsessed newspapers quickly produced tons of Meghan-and-Harry news, examined from every possible angle.

But if you read carefully you might find veiled traces of the racism and class-based snobbery that last year spurred Prince Harry to issue a highly unusual statement of indignation on Ms. Markle's behalf.

He was responding, for instance, to a Daily Mail report saying she was "Straight Outta Compton." In the statement, a spokesman for the prince denounced, among other things, "the smear on the front page of a national newspaper; the racial undertones of comment pieces; and the outright sexism and racism of social media trolls and web article comments."

But there was The Daily Mail back at it on Monday, explicitly pointing out that most of Prince Harry's previous girlfriends had been blonde, and going out of its way to make Ms. Markle's family back home sound like a bunch of eccentrically inbred rednecks.

"The extended Markle family is possibly the most unusual to marry into the House of Windsor so far," the paper said on its website. Her half brother, for instance, is newly engaged (to a woman named Darlene), "despite being arrested after pointing a gun at her during a drink-fueled argument," the article reported.

And then there's Ms. Markle's uncle Frederick, 75, who as leader of the "Eastern Orthodox Catholic Church in America," is known as "Bishop Dismas," the paper reported, and is said by a former disciple to preside over such a dwindling congregation that it is possible there are no worshipers left. (He is married, the paper said, to Theresa Huckabone, and lives with her and their 38-year-old son in a house in Florida that cost $80,000.)

Meanwhile, the conservative columnist Melanie McDonagh groused in The Spectator about Ms. Markle's left-leaning political views and unsuitability, as a divorcée, to be married in the Church of England. "Obviously, 70 years ago, Meghan Markle would have been the kind of woman the prince would have had for a mistress, not a wife," she wrote.

By contrast, writing in the left-leaning Guardian, the commentator Afua Hirsch spoke admiringly of Ms. Markle's politics and said that her addition to the royal family would force Britain to confront truths about race relations that it prefers not to discuss.

"One of the problems with the discourse in Britain today is the tendency to downplay racial difference," Ms. Hirsch wrote. "By contrast, Markle has owned and expressed pride in her heritage, speaking at length about the experience of having black heritage in a prejudiced society; of seeing her mother abused with the "N" word, of working in a highly racialized industry as an actor, and the identity struggle to which so many people who grow up as visible minorities can relate."

The paper's website was full of a range of comments reflecting a range of views: from readers who marveled at what this new development signifies for Britain and for themselves, from readers who hate the royal family and want it to go away, and from readers who do not care at all.

"I'd love to agree with this," wrote a reader named "Nyder," "but I have to point out that the current royal family have German heritage and it hasn't exactly led to English people viewing the Germans as their kin."

ANNA SCHAVERIEN CONTRIBUTED REPORTING.

Meghan Markle's Sheer Top Was a Sneaky Statement for a Royal Portrait

BY VANESSA FRIEDMAN | DEC. 22, 2017

MEGHAN MARKLE, the soon-to-be wife of the man who is soon to be sixth in line to the British throne, set off something of a controversy this week when the couple's official engagement photographs were released.

There were two portraits: a close-up of the two nuzzling romantically, diamond engagement ring carefully, if seemingly casually, exposed; and a more formal seated arrangement. At issue was Ms. Markle's choice of top for the second: a sheer black shirt embroidered with gold leaves over a long ruffled skirt. (Prince Harry wore a blue suit and tie.)

Given that this portrait was part of the record for posterity, the shirt had a bigger impact than one might have expected. It pretty much immediately became a symbol of how Ms. Markle, a biracial American (former) actress and activist, was going to approach her new role.

"You've never seen a royal engagement photo like this," one commentator wrote.

Indeed, in the context of official royal engagement photos, the choice was quite radical.

Not only did it look transparent, save for those strategic embroideries (it wasn't actually transparent, probably because it had been lined), it was fairy-tale formal and, as a couture gown, reportedly priced at 56,000 pounds, or $75,000.

Compared to, say, the engagement photo of Prince William and Catherine Middleton, which featured the bride-to-be in a pretty, conservative white day dress by Reiss, a British high street label, and framed her immediately as a newly accessible, down-to-earth kind of royal,

Ms. Markle's choice was labeled variously as "sensual" and "risqué."

But what it was, really, was a pretty big statement of difference. Which was presumably the point.

Not everyone was so thrilled. Some took offense at the transparent nature of the top, which they felt was not dignified enough for a royal. Others were upset about the elitist price of the dress. Ms. Markle has, since her engagement, become a singular mover of product — the coat she wore when she and Harry announced their plans sold out almost immediately — but the ball gown is in a different category.

Whether you like the dress or not, or felt it was appropriate or not, it all adds up to proof that Ms. Markle is pretty clear on her job.

Not only did she dutifully represent her country-to-be by wearing all British brands (sweater by Victoria Beckham, dress by Ralph & Russo), as opposed to the Canadian labels she has favored in the past, but she did so while simultaneously acknowledging the Cinderella nature of her romance, at least in the public mind, and breaking, ever so slightly, with tradition.

She represents, simply by background, a completely different kind of royal. This has both raised expectations for reform and made traditionalists nervous. The engagement photo doesn't shy away from either reaction; it underscores both. It also demonstrates that she is perfectly aware that everything she wears is going to be under the social media spotlight, so she might as well make it work for her.

Indeed, it's not just what she wears, but what anyone around her wears. Just before the portraits were released, Ms. Markle attended the queen's Christmas lunch at Buckingham Palace. Another guest, Princess Michael of Kent, who is married to the queen's cousin, came under fire from Britain to Australia for sporting what looked like a Blackamoor brooch on her coat.

The choice of accessory was widely seen a not-so-subtle slap at Ms. Markle, who has talked about her past experiences with racism. Whether Princess Michael thought her jewelry through or whether it was simply an extraordinarily tone-deaf choice, the piece, and the reaction to it, are a sign that even the smallest gestures are going to have a heightened import as the royal family adjusts to a modern identity. Far beyond Britain and the formal royal watchers, many have a special investment in this particular story and how it gets told.

If her future sister-in-law modernized, to a certain extent, the royal image by knocking it gently off its pedestal, Ms. Markle has the opportunity and, apparently, the aegis, to take it further. The destuffing of the House of Windsor is entering a new stage.

This is going to be fun.

Meghan Markle Is Going to Make History

BY VANESSA FRIEDMAN | NOV. 27, 2017

ROYAL WATCHERS, fairy tale lovers and proponents of the "special relationship" between Britain and the United States, let out your collective breath: Prince Harry, fifth in line to the British throne, famous flirt, recent spokesman for mental health and all-around paparazzi magnet, and his girlfriend, the American actress Meghan Markle, are engaged. And the British royal family has officially entered the 21st century.

If the marriage of Prince William and Catherine Middleton was a rare instance in which a commoner wed the heir to the throne, this royal wedding will herald the Windsors' (relatively radical, if expected) embrace of a divorced and biracial American. And you know what that means!

Not just that she will redeem the legacy of Wallis Simpson. But that she will become a symbol among symbols: one of the most-watched, obsessed-over women outside of Hollywood. And like so many of the women who marry into the royal family, she probably won't be heard very much but will often be seen, so what she wears is suddenly going to matter, and be chronicled, a whole lot.

The British fashion industry, on tenterhooks as it awaits the various outcomes of Britain's exit from the European Union, must be rubbing its hands in anticipation. Oh, the clothes her patronage can potentially sell!

It has already started.

The belted white coat that Ms. Markle wore for her official engagement appearance with Prince Harry outside Kensington Palace on Monday, by the Canadian brand Line the Label, set off a frenzy that was said to have crashed the website within an hour. (The brand is said to be renaming the coat "the Meghan.")

And there is a blog — Meghan's Mirror — that chronicles her every style choice. Vogue has a piece online titled "Meghan Markle's Stealth Shopping Style Is All the Black Friday Inspo You Need," while InStyle crowed "The Nordstrom Black Friday Sale Has Discounts on Meghan Markle's Favorite Denim Brand."

If she does that for jeans, just imagine what she could do for, say, day dresses — like the forest green frock with a bow at the waist from Italian label P.A.R.O.S.H. she wore for her BBC post-engagement interview (for those who don't know the brand, which is probably most people, the name stands for Paolo Rossello Second Hand, Paolo Rossello being the designer and second hand referring to the fact the line began by repurposing vintage garments). Along with whatever protocol lessons she is taking, she is going to have to decide what kind of style setter she wants to be.

Just consider the fact that not only does Catherine, the Duchess of Cambridge, tend to create an immediate buying frenzy for anything she wears, but so do her children: Prince George and Princess Charlotte. Consider that, with Theresa May in 10 Downing Street rightfully focusing attention on what she negotiates more than on the shoes she wears, there is no first lady equivalent à la Samantha Cameron, to boost the local fashion industry through appearances and strategic styling, thus upping the spotlight ante on the new-gen royals.

And consider that unlike Ms. Markle's future sister-in-law, who has been adept at walking the very fine fashion line between classic and accessible with her patronage of brands from the high-end (Jenny Packham and Temperley London) to the high street (Zara, Topshop, Reiss), always with a sensible pump (often by L.K. Bennett) and de rigueur sheer stockings, Prince Harry's bride will have a certain leeway. She can be more adventurous, less strictly appropriate.

That is both because her future husband is further from the responsibilities of the throne, and because the expectations surrounding them are different: their job, to a certain extent, is to push boundaries; to be even more relatable and modern than are Catherine and William.

JUSTIN TALLIS - WPA POOL/GETTY IMAGES

Pippa Middleton married James Matthews at St. Mark's Church on May 20, 2017. She wore a gown by the British designer Giles Deacon.

I mean: Ms. Markle did wear ripped jeans (ripped jeans!) to sit near her future husband at the Invictus Games in September in Toronto. It caused a hoo-ha, but as she began, so she may continue. Just imagine the big step forward she could take with bare legs. Certainly, the strappy Aquazzura stilettos she chose for her engagement debut were more daring than her sister-in-law's trademark footwear. Will she choose to champion certain British designers — perhaps, like Michelle Obama with American ones, the edgier and up-and-coming (Simone Rocha? J.W. Anderson?) — the better to promote them around the world and show her loyalty to her new country? Or will she underscore the values of cross-border relationships in the face of British isolationism, and work with some names from the United States? Those famous jeans were by the Los Angeles-based brand Mother, known for producing its denim in the U.S.A. Presumably, though she wore some Canadian brands while filming the television show "Suits" in

Toronto, as she did on Monday with LINE, she won't regularly continue, though it's possible the fact she did not choose a U.K. designer for her engagement look is telling. Will she work with a single designer, or spread her favor?

Burberry is about to name a new creative director (rumor has it that Phoebe Philo of Céline is the favorite). A new designer for a new royal, both fresh faces in heritage houses, would make for a very nice narrative. Or there's Victoria Beckham, another barrier-breaker, who moved from frothy pop stardom to designer substance, and could be a kindred spirit when it comes to crafting an image.

We will see — perhaps the front rows of London Fashion Week in February, where Ms. Markle will unquestionably be the most-desired guest for any brand, will provide a clue. Still, the first real statement as to where this is all going will be the wedding dress. There is a lot riding on the choice.

When Catherine opted for a gown from Sarah Burton for Alexander McQueen (one of the best-kept secrets of 2011), it spoke of her desire to support both a woman and a newish British brand, and it started an on-off partnership between the duchess and Ms. Burton that has continued to this day, and helped recast McQueen as more than just a high-fashion name known for intense creativity and a dark past. When her sister, Pippa Middleton, chose Giles Deacon as the designer of her wedding look in May, it likewise set off a frenzy of Deaconophilia.

Both women opted for Grace Kelly-like, lace princess confections, marked by simplicity and an implicit reference to that famous wedding past, with all its cinematic romance.

Ms. Markle has a chance to chart a new course via her dress, one that is perhaps a little more contemporary and a little less spun sugar. One that says to the millions who will be watching: This is the way I am redefining how it looks to be royal. Ms. Markle is someone who implicitly understands the power of dressing the part, so surely this opportunity has not escaped her.

Here's hoping she seizes it.

Can Meghan Markle Save the Monarchy?

OPINION | BY IRENOSEN OKOJIE | NOV. 28, 2017

LONDON — There were quiet rumblings in the press when they first started dating, a whiff of snobbery: Meghan Markle — half black, American, divorced, actress — was a curiosity. Perhaps it was a phase. There were comparisons to previous girlfriends, all of whom had been waifish blue-blooded blondes. There was a half-sister wheeled out, who declared Ms. Markle's past behavior to be "not fitting for a royal family member" and pitched a tell-all book to publishers. All of it came with the implication that Ms. Markle was an unlikely candidate to be taken seriously. She would never join the House of Windsor.

And yet, she will. In an announcement that went out Monday morning, His Royal Highness the Prince of Wales declared that Ms. Markle would marry Prince Harry in the spring. In the era of Brexit and Donald Trump — a time when we've seen an increase in racially motivated crimes, hateful rhetoric and fear mongering — Prince Harry's union with Ms. Markle is not only a bold antidote, it's astonishingly political (even if Ms. Markle, who has previously discussed the complexity of her identity as a mixed-race woman and says she has found the conversation about her race "disheartening," may not view it as such).

Admittedly, for the most part, until recently I'd been indifferent to the monarchy. It felt old-fashioned, an archaic and exclusive institution people of color couldn't really connect with nor would feel particularly invested in, given its long historical association with colonial projects.

Prince Harry openly and defiantly dating Ms. Markle made me, a black British woman, see the royals slightly differently. Suddenly they — or Harry, at least — seemed more open-minded. And it wasn't just me: Other women of color, too, I found, had begun taking notice and talking about the monarchy. Friends discussed the possibility of an engagement, whether the royals would be forward-thinking enough to give Harry permission. When the announcement finally came, the reaction from people of color on both sides of the pond was explosive; memes were deployed immediately.

Something was happening; not since Diana, Princess of Wales, has there been this kind of interest from young people in a member of the royal family.

Even before Monday's announcement, Prince Harry had exceeded Britain's expectations of him. Over the last few years, he'd matured from a mischievous, slightly unruly young man (his unclothed escapades on a laddish trip to Vegas in 2012 spring to mind) into the more mature version of himself we see today. There had been contrition, progress, a new level of comfort in his skin, a clearer sense of direction. He'd served in the military, created the Invictus Games, done charity work, all the while retaining a certain cheekiness, warmth and accessibility. He was the prince who took his duties seriously but didn't appear to take himself too seriously.

Now, with his engagement, Prince Harry has thrown the royal rule book on who can and can't be a princess out of the window. In his choice of partner, he has shown a certain courage, a propensity to do things on his terms. It is an act of royal rebellion nobody saw coming.

Are we being ushered into a new era where the boundaries of race and class will be blown open in Britain, when people will grow more open-minded about who they can consider as a mate? This is probably optimistic, though in some ways not: Interracial marriages are on the rise in Britain. In this sense, the prince and Ms. Markle are following, not leading. What is more intriguing is the question of whether, as a result of this unlikely pairing, more people of color will come to feel they have a stake in the country's most old-fashioned institution.

There have been some racist responses to the announcement, just as there were racist reactions when they first started dating. There will probably be more. It's impressive to see a prince who's not afraid to ruffle a few feathers, who has made a clear statement against those prejudices by refusing to allow them to affect his personal choices.

Harry feels millennial, current, like a prince for our times. His impact on modernizing the royal family's image cannot be underestimated. He's made the royals seem more in touch with the public. His union with Ms. Markle has shaken to the core the country's ideas about who is entitled to a seat at the royal table.

We live in strange times, with an American president who panders to right-wing hate, in a world that seems to have taken several steps backward. And so in these times, when a British prince goes against both royal and societal norms to propose to his biracial girlfriend, it's worth taking a moment to smile.

IRENOSEN OKOJIE (@IRENOSENOKOJIE) IS A NOVELIST AND SHORT STORY WRITER.

Prince Harry and Meghan Markle Invite Members of Public to Wedding Day

BY CEYLAN YEGINSU | MARCH 2, 2018

LONDON — Your invitation is probably not in the mail.

Prince Harry and his fiancée, Meghan Markle, announced on Friday that they would invite about 1,200 members of the public to Windsor Castle to celebrate their marriage in May.

The couple will welcome a total of 2,640 people to the grounds of their wedding venue to watch the arrival of the bride and groom at the chapel, which will be followed by a carriage procession from the castle, Kensington Palace said in a statement.

"Prince Harry and Ms. Meghan Markle have said they want their wedding day to be shaped so as to allow members of the public to feel part of the celebrations, too," the palace said.

Members of the public from across Britain and from various walks of life will be nominated to attend the celebration.

"The couple has asked that the people chosen are from a broad range of backgrounds and ages, including young people who have shown strong leadership, and those who have served their communities," the palace said.

The couple also invited:

- 200 people from a range of charities and organizations;
- 100 students from two local schools;
- 610 members of the Windsor Castle and St. George's Chapel communities;
- 530 members of the Royal Households and Crown Estate.

The Palace announced the couple's engagement in November, after Prince Harry proposed to Ms. Markle at his home in Kensington Palace, after a roast chicken dinner.

The wedding will take place on May 19 at 12 p.m. at Windsor Castle's 15th-century chapel. A reception for friends and family hosted by Prince Charles will follow.

The palace said last month that the archbishop of Canterbury, Justin Welby, would marry the couple, and that the Right Rev. David Conner, the dean of Windsor, would conduct the service.

The queen and other members of the royal family will attend the wedding, along with Ms. Markle's parents, Thomas Markle and Doria Ragland. The palace said it would release more details about the ceremony in the coming weeks and months.

A Mixed-Race Royal Couple?
It Wouldn't Be the First

BY MONICA DRAKE | NOV. 30, 2017

PRINCESSES FICTIONAL and real, from Cinderella to Sleeping Beauty to Princess Diana, all have in common skin as pure white as the driven snow.

Black girls, popular folklore suggests, don't grow up to be princesses.

The engagement this week of Princess Diana's youngest son Prince Harry to a biracial American actress named Meghan Markle delighted many African-Americans, who greeted the news on social media with increasingly rapturous gifs, memes and liberal use of all caps.

#blackprincess gained traction on Twitter and Instagram, with users celebrating Ms. Markle's African ancestry and the fact that Prince Harry's mother-in-law would be a dreadlocked black Californian. (For the record, Ms. Markle will probably be a duchess, not a princess.)

The reaction is understandable. Since the trans-Atlantic slave trade and colonialism created the idea of a single African race, the term "black princess" has been an oxymoron. The conception of black womanhood that scholars frequently cite — mammy, jezebel or sapphire — is antithetical to the idea of a princess, a cosseted women whose prince comes to sweep her off her feet and solve all of her troubles.

In fact, black women have become royals for years and years, unbeknown to many.

Some aristocratic families in Europe have already broadened the idea of what sort of spouse is acceptable, said Archduke Franz Ferdinand von Habsburg-Lothringen, whose great-great-great-grandfather was Emperor Franz Joseph I of Austria, king of Hungary. His wife, Archduchess Lei von Habsburg-Lothringen, is an African-American lawyer who grew up in the traditionally black New York City neighborhood of Bedford-Stuyvesant and in Columbia, S.C.

"For the modern Habsburgs," Mr. von Habsburg said in a telephone interview, "the importance of who your wife is is more about whom you have fallen in love with than how they fit into the aristocratic family." That he is an archduke rather than a count reflects his family's shift. In the past, he would have lost his title for his marriage, but now he and his wife have kept it and are presented in family gatherings as such. "The family modernized its rules to survive," he added.

He and Ms. von Habsburg are not the only mixed-race couple. Mr. von Habsburg's brother married a South Sudanese woman, and other European royals with black spouses include Prince Maximilian of Liechtenstein, whose wife, Angela Gisela Brown, is an Afro-Panamanian from New York City, and Christian Louis, Baron de Massy of Monaco, who married a Guadeloupian.

The history of black royalty, and of race itself, may be more complicated than contemporary mythology would suggest. One historian theorizes that Queen Charlotte, the wife of King George III (who ruled England from 1760 to 1820) was the descendant of a Portuguese royal family with African ancestry. He also suggests that Alessandro de Medici, the 16th century duke whose progeny inhabits royal houses across Europe, was mixed race.

And black women have, of course, married African aristocracy for millenniums and continue to do so.

The fact that those unions are not celebrated with such fanfare was not lost on critics. They noted that the progeny of an empire that transported Africans as chattel and occupied broad swaths of the Continent as a colonial power was being celebrated for marrying a person whose ancestors it likely subjugated.

But the vision of a black princess is alluring because it supplies a bit of escapism. African-American women still face a number of ills: We are more likely to have suffered from depression than white women but less likely to be treated for it, more likely to die from cervical cancer, and less likely to find our Prince Charming through dating apps, according to OKCupid.

The hunger for a black princess was only partly sated by fictional characters like Princess Tiana, the Disney character; Nella the Princess Knight, the biracial Nick Jr. character; and Lisa McDowell, the character who would go on to marry the prince of Zamunda in "Coming to America." Even the show "Scandal," in which Kerry Washington plays Olivia Pope, the daughter of a man so powerful that he controls the rulers of nations, is a royal drama delivered in the trappings of modern American life.

So is princessing all it's cracked up to be? Ms. von Habsburg, the American archduchess who married into Austrian-Hungarian aristocracy, said that she has a low-key life except for occasional formal large family gatherings in castles throughout Europe. And when she and her husband think of cultural clashes, Thanksgiving is what comes to mind rather than royal etiquette. (At one point, he asked for col-LARD greens, much to her amusement.)

"It's not an American princess fantasy, but an American opportunity fantasy," she said of her life. "Sometimes, in our communities, we don't get across that all children — children of color — have a right to experience everything in the world. If you are standing in a castle at a black-tie affair next to your husband, you belong there."

So, Meghan Markle, Are You Familiar With the Statute of Rhuddlan?

BY KIMIKO DE FREYTAS-TAMURA | DEC. 2, 2017

LONDON — What did the Statute of Rhuddlan in 1284 lay the basis for? Who or what is Vindolanda? Where is the National Horseracing Museum? Name two habits that may start a fight with your neighbor in Britain.

These and other rather esoteric questions are what Meghan Markle, the American actress recently engaged to Prince Harry, Queen Elizabeth II's grandson and the fifth in line to the throne, will have to master in order to become a British citizen.

Most Britons, even a prime minister, find them almost impossible to answer.

Meghan Markle visited Nottingham, England, on December 1, 2017, for her first official public appearance with her fiancé, Prince Harry.

Ms. Markle, who was raised in Los Angeles, plans to seek British citizenship after she marries Prince Harry, Kensington Palace confirmed. It is a lengthy process that culminates in a torturous citizenship test that costs about $65 and is typically flunked by one-third to half of the applicants.

The announcement prompted some British news outlets to pounce on her apparent ignorance of "Britishisms" on a television show last year.

"She only managed to get a measly four out of 15 questions about Britain right," The Mirror, a tabloid, said disapprovingly, adding that she did not know the British word for "sidewalk" and committed a cultural faux pas by venturing that Vegemite was more popular than Marmite. (The word is "pavement," and Marmite, a yeasty paste spread for bread, is a national treasure. Vegemite is the Australian equivalent.)

The citizenship exam "is really hard," said Julian Knight, a member of Parliament and author of "The British Citizenship Test for Dummies."

ANDREW TESTA FOR THE NEW YORK TIMES

The Union Jack hanging at Oxford Circus in London. Meghan Markle's entry into the royal family is raising questions about British identity.

"We have a really long history, and it could be really difficult to recall everything," he said.

Ms. Markle has "got to be swotting," he added, using British slang that, as she will someday come to understand, means "to study assiduously."

She is refreshingly open about how little she knows about her future adoptive country, let alone the British royal family.

In her first interview with Prince Harry, shortly after their engagement was announced on Monday, Ms. Markle confessed that she had not been wholly aware of her fiancé's royal lineage before meeting him. A mutual friend had set the pair up on a blind date, she said, adding, "The only thing I asked her was, 'Was he nice?' "

The exam she will take is known officially as the "Life in the U.K. Test," and it is required for anyone settling in the country or seeking to become a citizen (and, therefore, a subject of the queen).

Before taking the test, applicants must have been living continuously in Britain for at least five years and must pay an application fee of about £1,200 — that's $1,600 in the sort of currency Ms. Markle best understands.

A spokesman for Kensington Palace insisted that she intended to follow the process the same way as any other "American marrying a British citizen." Takers of the exam have 45 minutes to answer 24 multiple-choice questions about British traditions, customs and history, all of which are based on information in an official handbook published by the Home Office.

Apart from Ms. Markle, there has been a spike of interest in the exam as debates over identity have mushroomed after Britain voted last year to withdraw from the European Union, a process known as Brexit. That referendum focused mostly on immigration, and many voters who support Brexit say British culture is being diluted because of the bloc's policy of open borders between member countries.

In the 18 months since the critical vote, there has been much soul-searching across the island about what it means to be British.

The questions on the citizenship test, many Britons say, do not go far toward settling the issue.

In addition, they say, the quiz is unfairly difficult, an assertion that was borne out in a scattershot survey of Britons one recent afternoon that found many struggling to answer sample questions correctly.

"A what?" Peter York, a prominent social commentator, exclaimed. "What is the Vindolanda?"

"Is that a real question?" he asked, perplexed. "That's extraordinary."

Mr. York, who blithely describes himself as an English "purebred" ("no Welsh, Scottish or Irish components in me"), found the questions unsettling. "I don't think I'd be a British citizen," he said. "If they can keep me out, they can keep anybody out."

(The answer: Vindolanda was a Roman fort just south of Hadrian's Wall in northern England. Mr. York also got the question about the Statute of Rhuddlan wrong; it led to the annexation of Wales to England.)

A copy of Magna Carta, the cornerstone of the British Constitution, at Salisbury Cathedral in England. Former Prime Minister David Cameron once admitted having no idea what the words actually mean.

Mr. York said he preferred that foreigners study Alan Bennett, the prolific playwright; John Cleese, the comedian famed for the "Monty Python" series; and the punk band the Sex Pistols.

Gemma Page, 26, said British identity "comes more from ideas like tea and fish and chips." Her husband, Liam, said British identity "isn't a matter of how much you know."

Britain "is a mongrel country," he said. "Take tea and fish and chips. Tea comes from India and chips from Ireland. The only thing we can claim is the fish, and that's because we're surrounded by water. Being British is the values you hold. We try to be tolerant. We have free speech."

George Jupe, 87, a Brexit supporter, said being British was a question of feeling. "But what makes you feel it, heaven knows," he said, taking leave with a lively "Cheerio!"

According to a 2014 survey by YouGov, the pollster, more than half of 18- to 24-year-olds and a third of 25- to 39-year-olds failed the citizenship test. Some respondents answered that Hawaii was part of Britain and that National Insurance was used to pay for supermarket home deliveries.

Even some members of the Oxbridge-educated elite have demonstrated some surprising gaps in knowledge of the motherland. In 2012, David Cameron, then prime minister, told David Letterman that "Rule, Britannia!" — a rousing patriotic song often associated with Britain — was written by Edward Elgar. (It was Thomas Arne.)

The former leader also admitted to having no idea what Magna Carta, the cornerstone of the British legal and political system, actually stood for. (It means "Great Charter.")

The test "is pointless," said Michael Odell, the author of "The 'Call Yourself British?' Quiz Book." He wrote the book because his publisher, a Dutch citizen, was so upset at failing her British citizenship exam that she commissioned him to look into why it was so difficult.

The civil servants who come up with the questions are "completely out of touch with applied British history and culture," Mr. Odell said, as he sat putting together a mock exam designed for Ms. Markle, to be published by a British newspaper the following day.

"Whitehall boffins are trying to demarcate areas of knowledge and culture, trying to distill them into British identity, which is kind of amorphous," he added, using a British term for a nerdish expert.

And in spite of an abundance of arcane historical information, Mr. Odell said, there were few questions involving minorities. In one test, he said, there was only one related question: "Who was the first person to introduce curry in Britain?" (It was Sake Dane Mohamed, in 1810, who also brought shampoo to Europe.)

A more recent test, however, asked a couple of questions about the Vaisakhi festival, which marks the Sikh New Year, and the Muslim religious holiday Eid al-Fitr. (The answer to two habits that may start a fight with your neighbor in Britain? Putting out garbage bags when it's not trash day, and keeping an untidy garden.)

Whatever the questions, at least three-quarters of them must be answered correctly.

"If Meghan Markle can't get past me," Mr. Odell deadpanned, "the wedding is off."

Royal Engagement Seen as Symbol of Change, With Asterisks

BY PATRICK KINGSLEY | NOV. 28, 2017

LONDON — For many in the British news media, the engagement of Prince Harry to Meghan Markle, a divorced biracial American, reflected how egalitarian Britain had become.

"A divorced, mixed-race, Hollywood actress who attended a Roman Catholic school is to marry the son of the next king," began the lead editorial on Tuesday in The Daily Telegraph, a conservative newspaper. "Such a sentence could simply not have been written a generation ago."

It was a sentiment — with some notable cautions — that echoed across political and ethnic boundaries.

Afua Hirsch, the author of "Brit(ish)," a coming book about racial identity in Britain, said that as a mixed-race child she had found it hard to reconcile her British-ness with "the family at the apex of society," the racially homogeneous relatives of Prince Harry.

"That feels like that's really changed," Ms. Hirsch said on Tuesday. "There's someone I can relate to now."

But for Ms. Hirsch and other chroniclers of racial inequality in Britain, it is problematic to frame Ms. Markle's engagement as too seminal a moment. The symbolism of Ms. Markle's entry into a family that once shunned commoners, Catholics and divorced people — let alone nonwhites — does little to diminish structural racism across Britain, several commentators said.

"Markle is not Britain's Obama moment and shouldn't be covered as such," tweeted Reni Eddo-Lodge, the author of "Why I'm No Longer Talking to White People About Race," a new book about institutional racism in Britain.

On Tuesday, it was announced that Ms. Markle would — in addition to joining the Anglican Church — apply for British citizenship after marrying Prince Harry on an unspecified date in May in St. George's Chapel at Windsor Castle, the site of many royal weddings.

In response, a columnist for The Independent highlighted how Ms. Markle would find it far easier to gain citizenship through her husband, compared with the process other nonwhite immigrants face. Such immigrants are disproportionately more likely to fail the admission criteria than their white counterparts.

Across British society, the average black graduate earns nearly a quarter less than the average white worker, according to 2016 research compiled by the Equality and Human Rights Commission, an independent watchdog founded by the British government. The black unemployment rate is around twice as high as the white equivalent. Black people are significantly less likely to attend a top university, or reach a managerial position, than whites.

Black Britons are also disproportionately more likely to be in prison than African-Americans, whose incarceration rates are themselves disproportionately high, according to a parliamentary report published in September by a team led by David Lammy, a British lawmaker.

Ms. Markle's engagement "is a wonderful moment for modern Britain, and it is especially poignant for Britain's ethnic minority communities," Mr. Lammy said, because it "sends a very powerful message about what it means to be black and British in 2017."

But citing Britain's gaping inequalities, he added, "We should never confuse powerful symbolism with the systemic action still necessary to address persistent discrimination and inequality."

And against the background of Britain's vote to leave the European Union, a referendum that led to a rise in racial hate crime, others found even less reason to cheer the royal engagement.

"Brexit Britain is a deeply and increasingly xenophobic and racist society," said Priyamvada Gopal, a lecturer on post-colonial literature at the University of Cambridge, who had personally suffered a recent instance of racial abuse.

"We know that to be black in Britain is to be seriously disadvantaged in relation to educational and employment opportunities," she said in an email.

"Britain's major universities and media houses are overwhelmingly white," she continued. "Students have been agitating in recent months to have their curriculum acknowledge Britain's imperial past, something the country has signally failed to do except through dishonest celebrations of imperial legacies."

She added, "How exactly will the marriage of a privileged young woman of color to a British prince address any of this?"

Many black Britons are happy about the engagement, said Charlie Brinkhurst-Cuff, deputy editor of Gal-Dem, a website that publishes women of color exclusively.

But Ms. Brinkhurst-Cuff also expressed wariness about exaggerating the engagement's significance, partly because mixed-race people like Ms. Markle are often already considered "acceptable," Ms. Brinkhurst-Cuff said in an interview with the BBC. "We're sort of fetishized by the elite."

She added that if Ms. Markle "was darker skinned, it would be very unlikely that she would be marrying Prince Harry."

The plans by Ms. Markle, 36, to take up British citizenship and be baptized as an Anglican in the Church of England underscores how the royal union has shattered precedents.

Ms. Markle will be the first American to marry into the royal family since Wallis Simpson, the divorced socialite whose relationship with King Edward VIII triggered a constitutional crisis and prompted his abdication in 1936. The couple wed in 1937.

And it was only in 2013 that the law was amended so that members of the royal family could marry Catholics without losing their place in the line of succession. Ms. Markle, a Protestant, was not baptized as a child. She attended a Catholic girls' school in her native Los Angeles.

It is unclear whether Ms. Markle will renounce her American citizenship.

In the United States, the oath administered to naturalized citizens requires that they "entirely renounce and abjure all allegiance and fidelity to any foreign prince, potentate, state or sovereignty."

Federal law does not state what happens if a native-born American — like Ms. Markle — marries a foreign prince.

MEGAN SPECIA CONTRIBUTED REPORTING FROM NEW YORK.

British Royal Weddings and the Barriers That Fell With Them

BY CHRISTINE HAUSER | NOV. 27, 2017

ROYAL-WATCHERS have a new reason to celebrate. The British monarchy is set to stage its next royal wedding — starring an American.

Prince Harry, who is fifth in line to the throne, and Meghan Markle, an actress from Los Angeles, went public with their engagement on Monday and are scheduled to wed next spring.

Like previous royal nuptials, it is expected to be an eye-catching spectacle of pageantry, observing centuries of tradition carried through generations of knot-tying. But the coming union has also inspired feverish commentary that highlights the modernizing of the British monarchy.

The couple's relationship has been scrutinized since the news that they were dating emerged over a year ago. Last year, Prince Harry lashed out at the racial undertones of British tabloid coverage of Ms. Markle, who is biracial and divorced, as not being British enough for him.

As part of its coverage on Monday, the BBC ran an item asking other interracial couples in Britain to weigh in. The Daily Mail ran the couple's engagement photo opportunity past a "body language expert" who deduced that Prince Harry, 33, was "terribly awkward" and that the "easy confidence" of Ms. Markle, 36, would be good for him.

Here is a look at other royal weddings and some of the scrutiny that surrounded them.

WILLIAM AND CATHERINE

Prince William and Catherine, the former Kate Middleton, were married in April 2011. Viewing estimates for the ceremony hovered in the three billion range, with more than a million lining the route of the royal procession. Wedding fever carried across the ocean, with many American businesses and restaurants holding events to commemorate the nuptials.

The couple met when they were students at St. Andrew's in Scotland, and Kate's wedding to Prince William was unusual in the context of the royal family, because she was a commoner. Their marriage was seen as an example of how members of a new generation of royals were taking spouses of choice rather than of royal lineage after the marriage of Prince Charles and Princess Diana ended in divorce.

William and Catherine are expecting the birth of their third child in April.

CHARLES AND CAMILLA PARKER BOWLES

Charles, the Prince of Wales, and Camilla Parker Bowles were married in April 2005. It was the second marriage for both, and each had two children from the first marriage, all of whom attended the civil service and church blessing in Windsor.

The marriage made Camilla, his longtime mistress, the Duchess of Cornwall and wife to the heir of the throne. The wedding was a sign of how things had changed from the era when royals were not allowed to marry divorced people.

CHARLES AND DIANA SPENCER

Prince Charles's first marriage, to Lady Diana Spencer in July 1981, was called the "wedding of the century" by the tabloids and watched by an estimated 750 million people worldwide.

There were 2,500 guests inside St. Paul's Cathedral, with television viewers around the world witnessing what The Times described as a "fairy tale come to life" when the 32-year-old prince, in naval uniform, married the 20-year-old daughter of an earl.

The marriage vaulted Lady Diana into the role of a national emissary for Britain as the Princess of Wales as she threw herself into charitable work worldwide. The couple had two sons, Prince William and Prince Harry.

Prince Charles and Princess Diana separated in 1992 and divorced in 1996. Their union was overshadowed by Mrs. Parker Bowles's relationship with Prince Charles, described by Princess Diana to a BBC interviewer in 1996 as "three of us in this marriage, so it was a bit crowded."

Princess Diana died in a car crash in Paris in 1997, setting off a flurry of news coverage worldwide.

MARGARET AND ANTONY ARMSTRONG-JONES

Princess Margaret, the sister of Queen Elizabeth II, married Antony Armstrong-Jones in May 1960. Mr. Armstrong-Jones, a photographer, became the Earl of Snowdon. He took Princess Margaret's official portrait in 1958, and they connected again at a dinner party and began a secret affair.

The union was seen by many as a breakthrough in class barriers — Mr. Armstrong-Jones was the first British commoner in four centuries to marry a king's daughter.

EDWARD VIII AND WALLIS WARFIELD SIMPSON

King Edward VIII abdicated in December 1936 so he could marry his twice-divorced American mistress, Wallis Warfield Simpson. The Church of England opposed the marriage at the time, but the king chose love over his royal duties, allowing his younger brother to take his place as King George VI. Edward and Ms. Simpson were married in 1937.

As Prince Harry and Meghan Markle Wed, a New Era Dawns

BY ELLEN BARRY | MAY 19, 2018

WINDSOR, ENGLAND — A thousand-year-old English castle echoed with the exhortations of an African-American bishop and a gospel choir on Saturday, as Prince Harry wed Meghan Markle, an American actress, nudging the British royal family into a new era.

Ms. Markle, who has long identified herself as a feminist, entered St. George's Chapel alone rather than being given away by her father or any other man, a departure from tradition that in itself sent a message to the world. She was met halfway by Prince Charles, her future father-in-law and presumably the future king of Britain.

Prince Harry, who is sixth in line for the throne, has long called on Britain's monarchy to draw closer to the daily life of its people. But the most extraordinary thing he has done is to marry Ms. Markle, an American actress who is three years his senior, biracial, divorced and vocal about her views. Their choices at the wedding, many of them heavily influenced by black culture, made clear they plan to project a more inclusive monarchy.

In a time of tribalism and separation, it was a clear move toward an integrated modern future from the oldest of houses. Seated directly opposite Queen Elizabeth II was Ms. Markle's mother, Doria Ragland, the descendant of slaves on plantations in the American South.

In the knight's stalls supporting Ms. Markle, beneath rows of medieval swords and helmets, sat a constellation of American celebrities, among them Oprah Winfrey who, with a great gift for openness and emotional candor, has become an icon for black women.

There were the Hollywood and humanitarian megacelebrities George and Amal Clooney, and the tennis star Serena Williams. A gospel

Prince Harry and Meghan Markle kissed on the steps of St George's Chapel after their wedding in Windsor, England, on Saturday.

choir sang the Ben E. King song "Stand By Me," and the couple exited to the rousing civil rights anthem "This Little Light of Mine."

In short, it was not your average royal wedding. Among the throngs who filled the streets of Windsor on Saturday were black women who had flown in from Houston and Atlanta, moved, sometimes to tears, to see a woman of color so publicly adored.

"One of the children of slaves is marrying a royal whose forerunners sanctioned slavery; the lion is lying down with the lamb," said Denise Crawford, a court stenographer from Brooklyn.

"I just want to be here to observe the changing of the guard and the changing of the British Empire," she said. "Today is a day that history will never forget."

The most startling moments came with the sermon by the Most Rev. Michael Curry, the Chicago-born bishop of the Episcopal Church.

Bishop Curry, in the great tradition of black preachers, delivered a loose, improvisational sermon that began as a meandering discourse but built to a passionate, shouting climax, name-checking Martin Luther King Jr. and slave spirituals along the way.

"I'm talking about some power, real power," he boomed. "Power to change the world. If you don't believe me, well, there were some old slaves in America's Antebellum South who explained the dynamic power of love and why it has the power to transform."

At one point, seemingly sensing the passage of time, he said, "We're going to sit down; we gotta get y'all married."

He punctured the hallowed, starchy decorum of the day, visibly shocking some members of the royal family. Some suppressed giggles. Zara Tindall, a granddaughter of the queen, looked as if she might fall off her chair.

The episode delighted viewers on social media.

"A black reverend preaching to British royalty about the resilience of faith during slavery is 10000000% not what I thought I was waking up for, the royal wedding is good," Elamin Abdelmahmoud, social media editor at Buzzfeed, wrote on Twitter.

When the couple stepped out of the church and into the sunshine, a jolt went through the crowd, which cheered their first kiss as husband and wife.

For Britons, there was a sense of an old heartbreak being mended. Many people here feel a special affection for Harry, who was only 12 when his mother, Princess Diana, died in a car crash. On the day of the funeral, Harry was made to walk behind her coffin, and much of the country watched as his face crumpled.

"He was such a young boy," said Christine Janetta, 57, one of the charity workers invited to greet the couple from the lawn on the grounds of Windsor Castle. "We've all been very protective of Harry, because we saw that little boy with his broken heart."

Ms. Janetta said she was devoted to Princess Diana, and that she thought it would have given her a sense of deep relief to see her sons

TOLGA AKMEN/AFP/GETTY IMAGES

The carriage carrying Prince Harry and Meghan — now known as the Duchess of Sussex — made its way from the chapel.

happily settled. "He's just his mum," she said. "He is a carbon copy of his mum. Just look at the smile."

Harry's popularity helped give him the power to stretch the bounds of convention by marrying Ms. Markle, an American of mixed race. The decision may have a lasting effect on British society, which has been swept by a wave of anti-immigrant feeling. But it has not made things easier for the couple.

As the wedding approached, British newspapers swung the klieg lights of their attention to Ms. Markle's estranged half siblings, who said scathing things about a bride whom few Britons knew. More damaging were insistent approaches to her father, Thomas Markle, a retired Hollywood lighting director who declared bankruptcy years ago and now lives alone in Mexico.

A week before the ceremony, The Daily Mail reported that Mr. Markle had colluded with a photographer to stage seemingly candid pictures. With that, Mr. Markle dropped out of the wedding in

Doria Ragland, the mother of the bride, and Prince Charles and his wife, Camilla, leaving after the wedding ceremony.

disgrace, leaving Ms. Markle with only one blood relative, her mother, to attend the ceremony at her side.

On Saturday, royal fans embraced the couple unreservedly. People had camped out all night, huddling in blankets and clutching hot-water bottles, in hopes of making eye contact when the couple left the chapel. Along the main street of Windsor, people leaned precariously from windows.

Many of those lining the streets said they liked the change the couple represents.

"It's very good for the monarchy that Meghan Markle is a divorcée," said Christel Funten, a nanny, had traveled from Paris to attend the celebration. "It breaks a taboo. It's magnificent."

Charlotte Osborn, a Londoner, said the wedding showed how far the country had come since 1936, when King Edward VIII chose to abdicate the throne so that he could marry Wallis Simpson, a divorced American.

Prince Harry, Duke of Sussex, and the Duchess of Sussex depart for the evening reception at Frogmore House.

"It's a modern version of Wallis Simpson, where it all ends sensibly, rather than in disaster," she said.

Any royal wedding is theater, and this one did not disappoint. The dim vaulted opening of St. George's Chapel, whose construction was finished in the reign of King Henry VIII, was so densely crowded with meadow flowers that it felt as if you were stepping into a wonderland. A palace spokesman described the floral style as "cascading hedgerow," and it filled the chapel with the smell of growing things.

Harry arrived at the chapel on foot, walking beside his brother, Prince William, in the doeskin frock coat of the Blues and Royals, the regiment he joined after graduating from military school. Harry took his place in the chapel and shifted in his seat nervously, trying to catch Ms. Ragland's eye.

Ten minutes later, Ms. Markle stepped from a Rolls-Royce Phantom 4, in the company of two small pageboys in military dress. Her dress, with a flowing train 16 feet long, was dazzling pure white, wide-necked and minimal, leaving her collarbones bare, à la Audrey Hepburn.

The dress, which had been the subject of agitated speculation for weeks leading up to the wedding, was designed by Clare Waight Keller, the first female artistic director at the French fashion house Givenchy.

Prince Harry's popularity helped give him the power to stretch the bounds of convention by marrying Ms. Markle, an American of mixed race.

Seven tiny bridesmaids and pageboys trailed behind her, holding the edges of her 16-foot veil. As she approached the altar, she gave a quiet "Hi" to Harry. He flushed and, when she stood opposite him, added, "You look amazing."

Harry has decided to wear a wedding ring — a break from tradition not just for the royal family but for British aristocrats in general. Asked whether they would support the couple in their marriage, the guests said, "We will."

As a bride, Ms. Markle stood apart from Diana, a 20-year-old who nearly disappeared inside pouffes of meringue, and from Kate Middleton, now the Duchess of Cambridge, a school friend who had known William for 10 years at the time of their marriage, and was well known to the British public.

Mesha Griffin, an African-American schoolteacher from Washington, had flown to Britain alone, just to be present on the day of Ms. Markle's wedding.

"She is owning her heritage," Ms. Griffin said of the bride. "She is going to impact history in a way we saw with Princess Diana, not in a disrespectful way. She will respectfully change history."

Reporting was contributed by Stephen Castle and Iliana Magra from Windsor; and Sarah Lyall and Anna Schaverien from London.

CHAPTER 4

Much Ado About Royals

Royal weddings invite the public into an otherwise inaccessible institution. The public obsession with them stems from cultural, personal and historical nostalgia. The media and the memorabilia industries create coverage and products that capitalize on, and sustain, that nostalgia. To some, the royal frenzy is tiresome, outdated and misdirected. However, as the monarchy takes steps to modernize, the attention is likely to continue.

For an English Town, Wedding Madness and History

BY STEVEN RATTNER | JULY 24, 1981

B.J. BROAD, watch and clockmaker, has added commemorative teaspoons to his shop window. Across from it, on Hyde Lane, P.&J. Berry, clothiers, displays only red, white and blue garments, interspersed with wedding items. But neither can match B.V. & R.C. Hicks, who have turned their general store into an orgy of celebratory trinkets — mugs, plates, candies, booklets, pens, posters, cookie tins and even balloons.

Here, the birthplace of the last Englishwoman to marry an heir to the British throne, celebration of The Wedding, as the forthcoming nuptials of Prince Charles and Lady Diana Spencer have come to be known across the kingdom, is in full swing.

"It's different from the humdrum way of life," said Rosemary Hicks, who with her husband, sells just about everything from their comfortably cluttered store. "It livens up things a bit."

Excitement is nearly universal in this secluded town of about 8,500 on the edge of the Cotswolds. The various souvenirs are selling briskly, decoration of the village is expected to reach a peak this weekend, and one ecstatic homeowner has transformed his driveway gate into a Union Jack with the Prince of Wales's crest superimposed.

ANTI-ROYALISM IS IN RETREAT

Well off the tourist routes and unlikely to be the recipient of a royal visit, the celebratory zeal of Purton, an intimate cluster of a dozen shops, is motivated by utter delight. Prince Charles, extraordinarily popular here and across England, has raised his standing still further with his choice of Diana. Anti-royalism is in retreat in Britain these days.

"I think he's fantastic and I think he's made a super choice," said Reginald Herbert. "He's the first heir to the throne I've ever seen with his arm around his girlfriend like any pair of old lovers."

The delight stems as well from the fact that world attention will at last be on Britain for something it does well, for something other than its economic troubles.

"I'm thrilled to death about it," Edith Pearson said as she walked along High Street today, a wicker basket under her arm. "It's the one bright thing in Britain."

STRANGERS STAND OUT

To some extent, Britain's troubles have reached Purton. Like a small town in America, this Norman village where strangers stand out, is feeling modern pressures. The trains still roar through but have not stopped for 10 years. The brickyard, which had been the village's largest industry, closed five years ago. The populace, showing few signs of growth, is increasingly shopping in grimy Swindon, an industrial town four miles away.

Unsettled by the present, Purtonians cling tenaciously to the past. For them, the wedding is a hopeful sign for the future but perhaps, more prominently, a nostalgic reminder of Britain's greatness. Just a few residents know that Anne Hyde, who in 1660 married the man who was to become King James II, was born in a house now occupied by Americans. But they know almost everything else about the village and a Purton history quiz is under way, as a benefit for cancer research.

"Without a monarch, this country would be nothing," said Nelson Woolford, a machine operator, as he sipped bitter in Purton's Red House Club after his lawn bowling team lost to neighboring Malmesbury. "No other country can boast what we've done with royalty."

THE MAIN TOPIC IN PUBS

In pubs like The Angels and The Ghost Train, other favorite subjects of discussion, like sports and the weather, go on, but the wedding has assumed a central place. Tongues wagged reproachfully this morning at P.J. Webber's store (News agent, Tobacconist & Confectioner; Hardware, Paint, Electrical, Cycle Parts, Books, Cards, Patterns, Toys & Kits) over the decision of the King and Queen of Spain not to attend. Next door, at the combined post office and candy shop, lines formed as special wedding stamps went on sale.

For almost all Purtonians, the ritual next Wednesday was established weeks ago, when employers agreed to a special holiday. By 7:45 A.M., they will be glued to television sets, sandwiches and coffee close at hand. In early afternoon, a round of block parties will erupt across the village, to be followed in the evening by barbeques. Residents of Reids Piece, a small housing development, have already won a set of decorations from The Swindon Evening Advertiser for having planned the best celebration.

Of course, not everyone in the village is excited about the event. Mrs. Doreen Archer, the village librarian, plans to gather a half dozen friends and play bridge.

"People are very romantic," she said. "They don't look facts in the eye." But Pat Burgess, who thinks Diana was gunning for Charles for years, is having a friend videotape the event so she can watch it when she returns from vacation.

"My wife and children shall be inside glued to the television and I shall be outside in the garden," Duncan J. Bamford said. A group of Purton women signed up for a bus trip to London the night before the wedding to see the decorations and watch the fireworks. However, no one has signed up for a wedding day bus trip, reflecting a feeling that the coverage on television will be superior.

For Purton, the event will not be over on July 29. The next day, stores will begin sales of leftover souvenirs. And on Aug. 9, Peter Comley, a salesman of modest means, will present his wife Pat with a $470 Wedgwood commemorative wedding plate for her birthday.

Americans and Royalty: Symbols Clash No More

BY R. W. APPLE JR. | NOV. 5, 1985

THE IMMINENT VISIT of a young British couple, he 36 years old, she 24, has sent a frisson of excitement through Washington unmatched in the memory of old-timers in a city quite accustomed to receiving the glamorous and the celebrated.

The Prince and Princess of Wales are not due here until Saturday morning, but already the newspapers, magazines and television networks are outdoing themselves: What is their marriage really like? How much money do they earn for British business? Does she get along with her in-laws? How are they rearing their children? What are their political views, if any?

All of which leaves one larger question: Why do Americans care?

Washington, it is always said, is a city about power. The royal visitors have next to none and, even when Prince Charles inherits the British throne from Queen Elizabeth II, they will not have a great deal. Not as much as this Supreme Court Justice or that Cabinet member, each of whom would go unnoticed if they ever rode the subway.

Prince Charles sometimes complains to his intimates, in fact, that he has no defined role in life, at least not yet.

It cannot be simple glamour; the former Lady Diana Spencer is a beautiful woman, all right, although some Britons have been caddish enough to suggest that her nose is a bit too large or that she has become too thin, but other beautiful women come here without causing such a commotion. Not even Princess Grace of Monaco, who, after all, was royal, glamorous and American, stirred such a fuss.

Nor can it be money; there are plenty of American fortunes equal to the Prince's, if not to the Crown's, and plenty of American women with wardrobes that outdazzle the Princess's.

The answer is much more complicated, a compound of the obvious and the subtle. Youth and glamour and money matter, but so does tradition; it matters that Charles marches in the line stretching back to Victoria and Elizabeth I and William the Conqueror and yes, even George III. Not many institutions have the longevity of the British monarchy, and those that do are not easily personified.

Lacking a monarchy, lacking even an indirectly elected chief of state like West Germany's President, Americans gravitate toward the British monarchy, although some are made uncomfortable by dim 18th-century republican folk memories, which show up in a reluctance to bow or curtsy. That particular monarchy appeals to Americans because of a common language, because of cultural bonds, because of Britain's eminence among the countries that still have sovereigns, but also because people in the United States feel vaguely a part of it.

WATCHING AT THE PALACE

Each summer, tens of thousands of Americans stand outside Buckingham Palace, watching the changing of the guard, hoping for a glimpse of some member of the royal family. Ask why they are there and they will say, whether their names are Lombardi or Schultz or O'Brien or whatever, that they are touching base, "seeing where we come from," re-establishing the connection with Europe.

In a curious way, Americans feel closest to the country they rebelled against, and the hubbub over the royal visit is one sign of that.

Indeed, the visit is an attempt to capitalize on that emotion. At one level, the Prince and Princess will be here to publicize the "Treasure Houses of Britain" exhibition, and, not incidentally, to help persuade more Americans to visit the houses themselves. At another, they are here to promote British commerce, as witness the plan to visit a J. C. Penney store in suburban Virginia, which is not unconnected to the chain's nationwide Best in Britain merchandising campaign. At a third, they will hope subtly to reinforce the idea that Britain is America's staunchest ally.

FAMOUS FOR BEING FAMOUS

The final and crucial element in persuading ordinarily sensible people to pay so much attention to royal visitors is the passion for celebrity, which is one of the notable features of the times. In other eras, it was war heroes and great political leaders who were celebrated. Now Americans are fascinated, more than most peoples, by people with more ephemeral claims to fame, with fewer real achievements. The Prince and Princess are beneficiaries of this, as are football stars and television commentators.

But they offer much more to the celebrity-watcher. The actress's secrets may be prized out, but not the Princess's; as much as her sense of fun may seem to have "modernized" the monarchy, it really has not changed things at all. As Walter Bagehot observed in the last century, the monarchy's "mystery is its life." Only the Pope spends so much time in public yet keeps so much clothed in secrecy.

Thus, even when the Prince gives an interview, which is not often, he leaves doubt about his political views, and he seldom says anything pointed on any subject. When he does so, it is more newsworthy, more interesting than it would otherwise be. He suffers neither from the politician's overexposure nor from the vulnerability to dismissal from public office.

It may well be, as a recent Washington Post-ABC News Poll suggested, that most Americans have no clearly established opinion of the Prince or the Princess. But one need have no clearly established opinion of symbols to react strongly to them; they are by their nature not well defined, and yet they can be very potent indeed.

Gearing Up for Distant Royal 'I Dos'

BY ROBBIE BROWN | NOV. 18, 2010

MARIETTA, GA. — In this Atlanta suburb 4,200 miles from London, Tina Barnes is already planning a wedding-watching party. Never mind that the bride and bridegroom have not announced a date.

Ms. Barnes runs the Corner Shop, a little Union-Jack-patterned outlet that sells classically British items, from marmalade to mincemeat. "People who wouldn't normally stop in are coming by and asking, 'What do you think about the wedding?' " she said.

No one has to say which wedding. And what she, and other retailers across the country, think is that it will be good for the bottom line.

That became clear this week as Anglophiles and the companies that cater to them scrambled to stock their cabinets with every manner of kitsch — china, novelty rings, tea towels — bearing the smiling faces of Prince William of Britain and his fiancée, Kate Middleton.

Tina Barnes at her British store, the Corner Shop in Marietta, Georgia.

Not since the 1981 wedding of the prince's parents, Prince Charles and Diana, Princess of Wales, has the matrimonial side of America's "special relationship" shone quite so brightly.

Or so quickly. Even before the young couple could name the church (Ms. Middleton was reported to have toured Westminster Abbey), American morning shows were sending correspondents to Buckingham Palace. In New York, a British charity group, the St. George's Society, is making plans for a wedding-themed gala next spring aboard the aptly named Princess yacht. And a summer camp called Princess Prep that whisks young American girls away to British royal sites has received a flurry of phone calls and e-mails.

"We're definitely adding Kate to our list of princesses for this summer; we have to," said Jerramy Fine, 33, the camp's founder and a Colorado native.

To many Americans, a foreign wedding is even less relevant than the latest Lindsay Lohan bail hearing. But to others, the fairy-tale walk down the aisle "is the stuff our children's children's children will read in their history books," said Kerry Bamberger, the owner of British Wholesale Imports, a Los Angeles company scooping up and reselling Prince William coffee mugs and refrigerator magnets.

In New York, so many replicas of the couple's 18-karat sapphire-and-diamond engagement ring have been requested that one jeweler, the Natural Sapphire Company, says its Web site crashed under the traffic. The company's versions go for $1,000 to $2,000. The television channel BBC America is unveiling a slate of royalty-focused shows, including "Memories of a Queen" and "William and Harry," and TLC is rerunning its special "William & Kate: A Royal Love Story."

In Marietta, a customer in the Corner Shop on Thursday, Kari Puetz, 33, a chef whose family is English and Scottish-Irish, suggested that in a country without any royalty, Americans had claimed the British monarchy as their own.

Marisa Mace, the events manager for the St. George's Society, found her own equivalent: "They're young, they're famous — they're the same as Brad Pitt and Angelina Jolie, but with royal titles."

Toasts for Royals, Spiked With Scorn

BY ALESSANDRA STANLEY | APRIL 20, 2011

IT'S REMARKABLE HOW much malice is woven into the lacy specials and flowery tributes that are taking over the screen in the last days before the wedding of Prince William and Kate Middleton.

When Prince Charles and Lady Diana Spencer were married in 1981, television viewers behaved like doting, if somewhat nosy, guests. This time around, they are more like estranged members of the family — steeped in all the dazzle and expense, but not above whispering cattily about the canapés and betting on the happy couple's chances of divorce.

Diana's outsize, rock star celebrity cemented the American obsession with the British monarchy, but the fascination has turned ever more jaded even now, when a new and relatively untainted young pair is embarking on a royal fresh start. Television is going deliriously overboard, but after so many decades of telenovela scandal — lurid affairs, nasty divorces, Eurotrash spending sprees, tell-all books, sell-out interviews and, of course, Diana's fatal car crash in 1997 — there is a marked unwillingness to take this latest royal fairy tale at face value.

Instead networks are on a giddy, exploitative binge, spewing out shows — "How to Marry a Prince," "Royal Honeymoon Getaways," "Say Yes to the Dress: Princess Brides," "Modern Monarchy Dos & Don'ts" — that rubberneck all things royal, with a knowing leer. Countless networks and Web sites have carved out a niche, like the Food Network and its "Royal Icing Weekend," and Investigation Discovery, which plans to honor the Windsor wedding with a daylong marathon of "Who the (Bleep) Did I Marry?" on Saturday, a series devoted to newlyweds who discover that their spouses are bigamists, bank robbers or just big fat liars.

Newscasts keep daily countdowns to the wedding, which is on April 29, and most feature sneering British royal watchers and tabloid reporters. (NBC News offers a royal wedding app.)

Even cable networks like Wedding Central and OWN (Oprah Winfrey's new channel), which are not especially known for cynicism, put a premium on peeking behind drawn curtains and pointing out the cracks in all that gilt.

Despite the glut of programming, there is no shortage of would-be royal experts willing to say whatever it takes to get on television, including self-promoting members of the British aristocracy and the blogosphere's gossip king, Perez Hilton.

"I have heard from friends who have seen them out in a bar or nightclub that she does not leave his side," Lady Victoria Hervey says on "Kate: The New Diana?," one of many specials on Wedding Central.

Lady Victoria, a socialite-turned-reality show performer whom one British tabloid titled "the Was Girl," adds with a vulpine smile, "She was giving death stares to friends of mine or any girl that came near him, she was like, 'Block them off.' "

In this flood of documentaries, biographies, specials and memorabilia, perhaps the most benign depiction of Prince William and his future bride is in "William & Kate: Let Love Rule," a Lifetime made-for-television movie that was raced into production after their engagement was announced and will be shown several times before the actual wedding.

The production values are a little shoddy, but Ben Cross ("Chariots of Fire") does a surprisingly good impersonation of Prince Charles. Nico Evers-Swindell as William and Camilla Luddington as Kate are attractive and almost plausible, even in scenes where Kate, on a hunting trip, tries to win Prince Charles's approval. ("I think that solar power is the key to our future," she tells her future father-in-law.)

It's their story as told in official interviews and magazines like Hello!, with only a few references to less flattering tabloid reports. (Prince Harry is a bit of a bad boy, but he isn't shown donning a Nazi uniform for a costume party.)

But even as frothed up by Lifetime, this love story doesn't have much narrative juice: nobody, not even the queen, seems to mind that Kate is neither royal nor an aristocrat. The two met in college, dated for years, broke up, made up and didn't get engaged for another three years. "Waitie Katie" isn't the most romantic appellation; in the Lifetime movie version, the proposal immediately follows their reconciliation.

The real-life couple's lack of mystery may be fueling some of the scorn. The unhappily-ever-after finale to the gossamer wedding of Charles and Diana left a sour taste. And all those tabloid misadventures of Camilla, Dodi and Fergie cost the royal family a large part of its mystique and even its respectability. The royals have become celebrities that Americans can call their own, but in the New World, people don't always distinguish the Windsors from other storied dynasties like the Kardashians or the Judds.

Prince William's wedding has inspired scores of retrospectives of his parents' big day. But those memories aren't so gauzy — mostly they prompt acid flashbacks to the many ghastly moments, and people, that followed. Even James Hewitt, the former captain in the Life Guards cavalry regiment, who became known as "the Cad" after he published a tell-all book about his extramarital affair with Diana, is back. On "Kate: The New Diana?" he gives the new royal couple tips about discretion. "Don't allow your friends to talk, good or bad," Mr. Hewitt says.

He isn't the only former intimate taking a self-serving twirl in the reflected glory. India Hicks, who is a second cousin of Prince Charles, as well as his goddaughter, was one of Diana's bridesmaids, as she explains on many shows, including "Untold Stories of a Royal Bridesmaid" on TLC on Sunday.

Ms. Hicks, a former model who has a beauty and fashion business, interviews her own mother, Lady Pamela Hicks, who was a bridesmaid to Queen Elizabeth in 1947, about Diana. Biographers like Andrew Morton paint Prince Charles's young bride as a naïve innocent who did not get much support from Buckingham Palace. Lady Pamela does not agree.

"Diana was given endless lessons, she was given the queen's favorite young lady in waiting, but Diana didn't really want her, she had very strong ideas of her own," Lady Pamela says reprovingly. In comparison, Ms. Middleton comes out favorably. Lady Pamela noted that from what she had read about Prince William's fiancée, "she has strong ideas of her own but in a much more cooperative way."

As the wedding approaches, everybody on television seems to know the bride and groom better than they know themselves.

On "Prince William and Catherine: A Royal Love Story" on OWN, Ashley Pearson, an American entertainment reporter, explains that Ms. Middleton shrewdly made Prince William fall for her by donning sexy lingerie for a charity event. But her praise is faint. "For all that has been said about Kate's somewhat dull, maybe somewhat pedestrian personality," Ms. Pearson says, "the girl knows how to get attention when she wants it."

All this American lèse-majesté appears to have led to a backlash on the other side of the Atlantic. The British may have lost much of their reverence for the monarchy, but they don't seem too tickled when Americans flaunt their disrespect. BBC America has its own battery of wedding films and specials, and a few of them seem designed to put Americans back in their place.

"Royally Mad," for example, is a reality show in which five humble, ordinary Americans who consider themselves royalty buffs are invited to London, ostensibly to compete to see who knows more about the royal wedding, but mostly to make their British hosts look superior.

These somewhat dumpy out-of-towners are taken around by a tall, willowy former model and current television personality, Cat Deeley ("So You Think You Can Dance"), who cheerfully condescends as she escorts them to one of the couple's favorite nightclubs, Mahiki, and to Westminster Abbey. (Rich, the only man in the group, drops down and kisses the ground where Ms. Middleton will walk to the altar.) They also meet Prince William's polo instructor, who finds their childlike awe and eagerness amusing, up to a point.

British commentators love to make snarky remarks about Ms. Middleton's undistinguished roots, particularly her mother's career as a flight attendant. On "Prince William and Catherine," the OWN documentary, Lucie Cave, the editor of the gossipy British magazine Heat, snickers as she recounts the oft-repeated story of William's snobbier friends whispering "Doors to manual" whenever Kate walked in.

There is something even worse that royal watchers in Britain can say about Ms. Middleton, and Celia Walden, a columnist for The Telegraph, put her finger on it during a recent and somewhat saucy "Today" show segment on the bride's "magazine perfect" styling.

"She's looking very American, actually," Ms. Walden said with a smirk. "She's got that American gloss, I think."

That is possibly the most insulting thing you can say about a future member of the British monarchy. But it's also what makes this royal wedding the ultimate must-see moment on American television.

In Media's Wedding Frenzy, Hints of Viewer Fatigue

BY RAVI SOMAIYA | APRIL 22, 2011

LONDON — When Prince William and Kate Middleton emerge from Westminster Abbey as a married couple next Friday, they will be greeted by hundreds of reporters from around the world. But as the day draws near, there are signs that the media frenzy may outpace interest in the United States, and some disdain is appearing among the British as well.

The latest New York Times/CBS News poll, of 1,224 Americans, has found that only 6 percent of respondents have been following news about the wedding "very closely," and another 22 percent "somewhat closely."

Though a third of women under age 40, and 4 in 10 of those 40 and up, said they were keeping track of events, half of the male respondents said they were not following the buildup at all.

Anchors, reporters and support staff from American networks and cable news channels are already arriving here. And in the days leading up to the wedding, Buckingham Palace has promised to keep its floodlights on an hour later, until midnight, so that the palace can be used as backdrop for live news reports by television networks in the United States.

Broadcast networks are remaining tight-lipped about how extensive their coverage will be. CBS and NBC said they did not discuss staffing decisions; ABC did not respond to messages.

But three employees at NBC News, who spoke anonymously out of concern for their jobs, said that NBC and MSNBC would have about 200 people involved in covering the wedding. The large numbers were prompted, suggested one, by "the thinking that it's a happy, fairy-tale story — and America needs happy stories right now."

Some Americans, though, rejected that idea when contacted for a follow-up interview after The Times/CBS poll.

"It's their British thing, it's their custom," said Edward Rakas, 57, of Colchester, Conn. "I guess they enjoy it, but it's just not something I'm interested in."

Even in Britain, where hundreds of thousands are expected to fill London on the wedding day, a significant number — about 47 percent in a telephone poll conducted by Ipsos MORI last week — said they had little or no interest in the proceedings.

Some of that might be attributed to the contrast of a wedding steeped in centuries of opulent privilege with sweeping spending cuts that the government says are necessary to tame Britain's deficit. When it was announced in November that Prince William was engaged to Miss Middleton, one reader of The Daily Mail, which is usually staunchly royalist, commented, tongue in cheek, that the princess-to-be "has been largely unemployed since she left school and is now marrying someone who has been on welfare most of his life." With cuts to state benefits inevitable, the reader went on, "I do worry for them."

And in contrast to the ranks of earnest souvenirs that now fill London's tourist shops, disaffected Britons can also buy royal wedding airsickness bags.

Lydia Leith, the graphic designer behind the bags, said in an interview on Friday that she was inspired to make them after conversations with people who said they were "sick of the royal wedding."

She estimates that she has sold about 8,000 since February, adding, "I haven't really had time to count because I am just about keeping up with orders." Large quantities have been bought, she said, for anti-wedding parties that will be taking place around the country on Friday.

Many of those parties were organized by Republic, a group that has campaigned for the abolition of the monarchy since 1983, according to Graham Smith, its executive officer. "We've seen roughly a doubling of our numbers since the engagement was announced in November," he said, "to about 14,000."

Mr. Smith hopes that the wedding will help rally others sympathetic to his cause; the MORI poll showed that 18 percent of Britons would like to see the end of the monarchy.

"While we're all tightening our belts," he said, "they are helping themselves to our tax money for a big wedding."

The American media, said Fred M. Leventhal, emeritus professor of British history at Boston University, "does not have to worry about constitutional or financial elements."

Instead, he said, "It's fascinated with things royal partly because they're different from what we have. The glamour that attaches itself to some presidents, like Kennedy and to a lesser extent Obama, is politicized, and many people don't go along with it. The royal family are exotic, and they're free from all those conflicted political questions."

But when British royals toured the United States in 1939, he said, "they deliberately did not include most of the Midwest, because they felt there was general indifference."

More than 70 years later, he said, "it seems likely there will be large parts of the country that are indifferent this time, too."

MARJORIE CONNELLY CONTRIBUTED REPORTING.

Books, Brioche and Baby Clothes: The Royal Merchandise

BY JULIA WERDIGIER | JULY 22, 2013

LONDON — British retailers, hotels and ceramic factories are betting on the arrival of the royal baby to improve the otherwise gloomy economic situation.

Dave Lockett, the owner of Edwardian China, a pottery manufacturer, said his company would paint the name and date of birth of the new royal on more than 10,000 commemorative plates and other ceramics that were prepared weeks ago.

"We made them pretty generic so that it could be either a boy or girl," said Mr. Lockett, who hired extra staff to cope with the order load. "Then it was just a matter of waiting for the big day."

Britons are expected to spend more than £243 million (or $420 million) on merchandise, other goods and party food in July and August to celebrate the royal baby, according to the Center for Retail Research. That would compare with £163 million spent on souvenirs alone for William and Kate's wedding in April 2011.

Not knowing the name or gender of the royal baby has not prevented retailers from already selling royalty-inspired teacups, baby clothes and sweets. The department store Harrods has been selling a cup and a plate with the gender-neutral message "The first baby of the Duke and Duchess of Cambridge 2013." One online retailer is selling a royal baby pacifier while another is promoting a purple velvet diaper cover by saying that it was "inspired by royalty" and that "pretty soon Kate and William will be sleep deprived, too."

Krispy Kreme is selling doughnuts with white baby feet glazing, and Roberts Bakery, a British family-owned brand, created a special brioche for the occasion. The loaves, with a gold leaf crust and dried apricots, glazed cherries and pineapple inside, costs £30 each to produce, the company says, and will be given away to 50 winners of a contest once the baby is born.

Bookstores are also hoping for some royal help. "Shhh! Don't Wake the Royal Baby," by Martha Mumford, tells the story of a baby who just cannot fall asleep in the hustle and bustle of Buckingham Palace.

Benedetta Fullin, marketing manager at St. James's Hotel in London, said the hotel's special offer for royal baby showers has been "very popular, with about two baby showers thrown per week so far this month." The offer includes a Ralph Lauren gift voucher and a spa treatment for mothers-to-be.

For £10,089 for three nights, new parents can stay in the nursery suite at Marriott's Grosvenor House hotel in London. "Designed with a royal baby in mind," the hotel says the package includes one evening of child minding and a "dedicated baby concierge" to deal with emergencies such as extra nappies.

But not everyone has been as excited about the arrival of the royal baby. About 82 percent of Britons don't plan to celebrate the infant's arrival in any way, according to a poll of more than 8,000 people by Kantar Retail. "We fear that projections of a robust boost to the retail sector arising from the birth might be wide of the mark," Kantar said, adding that the amount of 2012 London Olympics merchandise that remained unsold "suggests that British shoppers might be suffering from event fatigue."

Helen Dickinson, director general of the British Retail Consortium, said that even if consumers fail to flock in large numbers to buy baby merchandise, the royal baby — like the recent sunny weather here — might still help Britain's economy by making consumers feel better. "The temporary lift in the general mood helps," she said.

Celebrity Weeklies Are Reveling in a Royal Baby, and Sales

BY CHRISTINE HAUGHNEY | AUG. 11, 2013

CELEBRITY WEEKLIES reported large declines in newsstand sales for the first half of the year, according to figures released last week, but editors didn't let the numbers get them down. They were too distracted by baby news.

The July 22 birth of Prince George brought these publications millions of readers eager for news about everything from Prince George's nursery and astrological sign to Prince William's paternity leave. And royalists and fashion watchers devoured news about Kate Middleton's first days of motherhood.

For the struggling weeklies, the royal baby has become the story that keeps on selling. People, which published the first royal baby cover with the "Royal Baby Joy!" collector's issue, was expected to sell 1.4 million copies during the two weeks it remained on newsstands, said Larry Hackett, People's managing editor. He added that it was the magazine's best-selling issue so far this year. And the issue released a week later, with the cover "First Days Home," was expected to sell a million newsstand copies. While Us Weekly missed getting the first royal baby photographs on its Aug. 5 cover, Mike Steele, editor in chief of the magazine, said he expected that the Aug. 12 cover, "Kate's First Week," would sell about 450,000 copies.

"There's definitely been a royal baby boom," Mr. Steele said. "Our readers love Will and Kate. They're unique among public figures because they're 100 percent likable."

Royal baby watchers also helped lead to record traffic on celebrity Web sites. People reported that the number of unique visitors to its Web site on the day Prince George was born and the day he left the hospital was 46 percent higher than average. On Prince George's birthday, unique visitors to People's mobile site jumped by 70 percent. While most People Facebook posts generate about 1,000 "likes," the royal baby prompted 22,000 likes for the magazine.

Both Us Weekly and HollywoodLife.com experienced their best month for Web site traffic in July because of the royal birth. Mr. Steele said Usmagazine.com recorded the most traffic in its history on July 23, the day Ms. Middleton left the hospital. ComScore reported that the magazine's Web site had 9.9 million unique page views in July, not including traffic from mobile devices. HollywoodLife.com, which is run by the former Us Weekly chief, Bonnie Fuller, attracted 4.6 million page views in July, according to comScore. "Kate Middleton" became the No. 1 searched keyword for the Web site that month, Ms. Fuller said.

Two photo galleries of the baby and William and Kate with the baby attracted more viewers than the Oscars. Stories about Kate Middleton breast-feeding, her breast-feeding wardrobe and how Carole Middleton is helping her daughter with the baby all were top performers.

"The moment that they announced the birth, traffic soared and didn't stop," Ms. Fuller said.

Then there are all of the companion products that come with a royal birth. Mr. Steele said the $9.99 so-called bookazine Us Weekly had been selling on newsstands about preparations for the royal baby had a boom in sales after the birth. Mr. Steele expects to publish another $9.99 special issue when Prince George's official photos are released. People has added mention of the prince to its subscription insert cards.

"This is for us what we think will be a new franchise," said Mr. Hackett about Prince George coverage.

Royals have long been a draw for celebrity magazines. Five of People's best-selling covers in its 39-year history featured royals, according to a spokeswoman, Kathryn Brenner. Princess Diana's death cover was the second-best-selling cover in the magazine's history, behind the magazine's 9/11 cover. The 2011 royal wedding propelled the best-selling issues that year for both People and Us Weekly.

But a new member of the royal family has added a new line of reporting for celebrity titles. Ms. Fuller said that her Web site's "HollyBaby" editor would oversee Prince George coverage.

"The royal baby will become a regular beat, just like Shiloh and Suri were the babies of six years ago," Ms. Fuller said, referring to the daughters of Angelina Jolie and Brad Pitt and Katie Holmes and Tom Cruise, respectively. "The two babies that Hollywood Life audiences are going to be obsessed with are going to be Prince George and Kim Kardashian's baby, North West."

Since Prince George left the hospital, even incremental stories have broken Web viewership records. Ms. Fuller said that a recent article about Prince William giving his wife a diamond brooch as a "push present" was on track to become the most-read article of the day.

Mr. Hackett has his sights set on the readership that will follow the release of official baby photographs.

"If history is any guide, they will eventually pose with the baby," he said. "That to me is a whole other opportunity."

Those interviewed agreed it was too early to compare readers' interest in the birth of Prince George with the interest in the baby born to Ms. Kardashian and Kanye West.

"Her baby has not been seen yet and there has not been a photo op," Ms. Fuller said. "There's no baby photos and Kim in fact has not been seen since she gave birth. So we don't have a comparable number."

Mr. Steele from Us Weekly said timing allowed the royal couple to out-Kardashian the Kardashians. Ms. Kardashian had her baby at 4 p.m. on a Saturday, while Ms. Middleton had her baby on a Monday during the workday and brought him home on a Tuesday when people were at their computers.

Major Royal News.
Impose Story of Your Choice.

BY SARAH LYALL | DEC. 3, 2017

IT WAS THE SUMMER of 2013. I was moving back to New York after 17 years as a London reporter for The New York Times. The house was a lonely wasteland of packed boxes and little bits of useless detritus. I had a one-way ticket home.

But a major news story was brewing, and word wafted down from the upper echelons of the newsroom: I was not allowed to leave the country until the very pregnant Duchess of Cambridge, the person formerly known as Kate Middleton, gave birth to the next heir to the British throne. And so I joined hundreds of representatives from the world's great (and less great) news media outlets, all of us waiting around for an event that, when it finally happened, was recorded by the satirical Private Eye magazine as: "Woman Has Baby."

Even readers of a serious newspaper in a country that long ago violently declared its independence from monarchs with English accents, it seems, love royal stories. Whenever we write them, as we did earlier this week when Prince Harry, fifth in line to the throne, announced his engagement to the American actress Meghan Markle, they jump to the top of the paper's "most viewed" and "most emailed" lists.

Though I spent only a small percentage of my time in London covering the royals, I was there for many of the big-ticket events: the breakup of the marriage between Prince Charles and Diana, the Princess of Wales; Diana's death; Charles's remarriage; and assorted other occasions of interest and intrigue.

Part of the reason readers gravitate toward those stories, I think, is a latent fascination with the idea of upper-class Britain as a refined throwback to a simpler, more snobbishly hierarchical age — the same thing that makes television shows like "Downton Abbey" and "The Crown" such guilty pleasures. Part of it is that at a time of bewildering change, the Windsors represent reliability and continuity. No matter what happens, there they are.

Also, because there is so little material of any substance to go on, because the public is allowed to see only public events — a princess gets married, a duke gets divorced, a prince gets a job as a helicopter pilot, the queen uses the phrase "annus horribilis" in a speech — we impose on them any narrative we like. We use them as prisms for discussions of privilege, of class, of tradition, of race (in the case of Ms. Markle), of what Britain was and what it should be. We examine them through their sometimes parasitic, sometimes symbiotic relationship with the British news media, which treats them at times as if they were little more than upper-crust Kardashians.

Covering the British royal family isn't like covering a normal family. You're not going to get anything out of them. They're masters of the no-content remark. Their public appearances are tightly controlled, and their activities most days — showing up at charity events, making boring remarks and leaving — are not in themselves raucously exciting to behold. When they give interviews, it's usually to British news organizations, and always under the most anodyne of circumstances.

And of course they're not our royal family, so it's hard to regard them with anything like the awe they provoke in pro-monarchy Britons. (Many Britons, of course, wish they would just go away.) I've met a few of them, and I can report that they are much as you might imagine, only more so.

Once, at a meet-the-princess lunch, I watched Diana reduce a bunch of seasoned (male) American foreign correspondents to spineless blobs of obsequious jelly competing to express their sympathy for how hard her life must be and bragging about how arduous their jobs were. ("Richard Gere is renting a house down the street from me, and so I can see something of what you must go through every day with the paparazzi," said one. "I work for a newspaper in Los Angeles, and have to write on deadline with an eight-hour time difference," said another.)

My favorite royal encounter happened to an American friend some years ago. It was at a fancy party outside London at which the queen was a surprise guest. My friend had not yet had dinner, but she had had several glasses of Champagne.

A receiving line formed. The queen stood next to an aide whose job it was to whisper in her ear a little tidbit about the identity of each new person, including where they come from.

"I understand that you're from Texas," she said, as the line moved along. My friend, addled by drink and confused by the queen's clipped accent, thought she said "Have you paid your taxes?"

And so she responded the way any American would, when asked such a personal question by a British monarch. Looking at the queen with her best republican expression, she declared, "No taxation without representation!"

And that was the end of the conversation.

Do Americans Love the British Royal Family? Quite

BY LIAM STACK | DEC. 4, 2017

THE ENGAGEMENT OF PRINCE HARRY and Meghan Markle last week inspired a wave of news coverage and online excitement. And that raised a question that comes up every time a British royal does something big: Why do Americans care?

After all, as an op-ed in The Washington Post argued recently, the founding fathers "violently overthrew our tea-sipping stamp-taxing overlords in large part so that we should not have to genuflect in front of the altar of royal bloodlines." Right?

Yet Americans do love a British royal wedding. In 2011, they reacted with similar excitement to the wedding of Prince William and Kate Middleton, and to the births of their children that followed. These bouts of monarch-mania in the former colonies have played out in a pop-culture environment shaped by imported shows like "Downton Abbey" and "The Crown."

British programming, long a staple of American public television, has spread to online services like Netflix, Britbox and Acorn TV. Indeed, from "The Great British Bake Off" to the creeping adoption of British slang, we appear to be living in a golden age of American Anglophilia, or an affection for the English and their ways.

Interest in the House of Windsor may be the most distilled version of that trend. President Obama even remarked upon it in 2015.

"I think it's fair to say that the American people are quite fond of the royal family," Mr. Obama said during a White House visit from Prince Charles. "They like them much more than they like their own politicians."

(Prince Charles politely disagreed, but a survey by the polling firm YouGov suggested Mr. Obama was right, depending on which American politician and which British royal the respondents were asked about.)

So what is the appeal? Observers of American Anglophilia say it is complicated.

Tom Sykes, an Englishman in Dublin who writes about the royal family for The Daily Beast, described the royals as the ultimate celebrities, albeit ones with "some meat on the bone."

"I do think if you're going to be interested in celebrities you don't know," Mr. Sykes said, "the royal family are probably more interesting people to be interested in than the Kardashians, say, because of the thousand years of history behind them."

The era of prestige television has helped cultivate and encourage these trans-Atlantic tastes by making escapist fare instantly, and repeatedly, accessible in a way that rental VHS versions of "Howards End" were not for an earlier generation.

Streaming services have helped introduce Americans to shows like "Downton Abbey" and "The Crown," turning them into critical darlings and bestowing American celebrity upon their British stars, like the actors Michelle Dockery and Claire Foy.

Not all successful British shows in the U.S. focus on the elite (hello, "Fleabag" and "Chewing Gum"). But the interior lives of the aristocracy, especially the royal family, have been particularly popular, from 1990s films like "The Remains of the Day" and early 2000s hits like "The Queen."

Glamour and escapism are a big part of the allure. It also helps that the British royal family — which received $57.6 million in taxpayer money during the 2016 to 2017 fiscal year — does not play any formal role, ceremonial or otherwise, in American life.

And while the monarchy may be the most popular institution in British public life, some in Britain criticize it as out of touch, said Suzanne Mackie, the executive producer of "The Crown," whose second season begins this week.

"There would probably be an apathy, an ambivalence, and some people would even be ill-disposed to them symbolically in what they represent," said Ms. Mackie, who is British. "So it's always interesting to us to counter that with the American relationship with the royal family and interest in the royal family."

Ms. Mackie attributed the royal family's appeal, in part, to "the mystique, the mythology around the throne and the monarchy." But for Americans, not just any royal will do. The August wedding of Prince Phillip and Danica Marinkovic in Serbia made barely a ripple in the United States.

"Americans are particularly interested in the British monarchy, it's not just monarchy in general," said Arianne Chernock, a historian at Boston University. "You don't see the same kind of interest directed at the Japanese Crown. I think it is about this special relationship, at root."

And so the engagement of Prince Harry to a biracial actress (Ms. Markle's mother is African-American) was celebrated as a moment of inclusivity, even though the House of Windsor is not even the first in Europe to welcome a black princess or duchess into the royal family.

Anglophilia in the United States dates back to "almost immediately after the American Revolution" ended British rule in the 13 colonies, Ms. Chernock said. "There is a desire to retain that strong cultural tie, and I think that persists to this day."

It is a feeling that has long cut across the social divide. In 1860, when Albert Edward, the Prince of Wales, visited the United States on the eve of the Civil War, hundreds of thousands gathered to see him in cities from Boston to Richmond, Va., which would soon be the secessionist capital, said Elisa Tamarkin, a scholar at the University of California, Berkeley.

"The love of this 18-year-old traveling prince was described as a universal feeling," Ms. Tamarkin said. "South Carolina had committed to secede if Abraham Lincoln wins, his winning was assured, Wall Street was in a panic, but the Prince of Wales was actually on the cover of Harper's Weekly five times in six weeks."

Prince Harry Is Getting Married. Time for Themed Mugs and Nightclub Tours.

BY AMIE TSANG | DEC. 24, 2017

LONDON — The cameras had barely finished flashing on the newly engaged Prince Harry and Meghan Markle. But Emma Bridgewater, a British ceramics manufacturer, was already making a mug to commemorate the royal moment.

The next week, just under 1,000 mugs — with "Harry & Meghan are engaged," and the date of the announcement on them — were on sale. They retailed online for around 20 pounds, or $27, and sold out within 24 hours.

From crockery emblazoned with official portraits to solar-powered toys with the queen's characteristic wave, Britain's monarchy is big

CREDITANDREW TESTA FOR THE NEW YORK TIMES

Goods on display at the Emma Bridgewater store in London.

Royal collector Margaret Tyler at her home in northwest London.

business. And that royal economy, normally catering to tourists and enthusiasts, kicks into high gear around major events.

"It's a flash of color in a rather gray world," said Emma Bridgewater, the eponymous founder of the ceramics company.

Britain's royal family will contribute an estimated £1.8 billion to the country's economy this year, according to Brand Finance, a consulting firm. The bulk of that was £550 million from tourism. Brand Finance estimates that travelers in town for Prince Harry's wedding, scheduled for the spring, will bring an additional £500 million next year. Roughly one-tenth of that amount is expected to come from merchandise sales. Enthusiastic collectors like Margaret Tyler are a discerning audience.

A dedicated royalist, Ms. Tyler, 73, has filled her home in northwest London with commemorative items, including a copy of the Issa dress that Kate Middleton wore during the announcement of her engagement to Prince William, and a little glass dish with a picture of Queen Elizabeth II that started her collection. One of her rooms is dedicated

One room in Ms. Tyler's home is dedicated solely to Princess Diana.

to Princess Diana, and another to the queen, which she rents out for £75 a night. Insurers have valued her collection at £40,000.

"I would like nice proper bone china stuff," Ms. Tyler said of the merchandise surrounding the latest royal wedding. "I don't buy everything. I've got to like it."

Royal fever is a capitalist tradition in Britain.

Royal Crown Derby, a porcelain manufacturer, has been making commemorative products since the coronation of King George III in 1760. Jan Hugo, a 59-year-old collector with 10,000 pieces who is based in New South Wales, Australia, has teapots dating back to Queen Victoria's reign.

"I think they just look for an excuse to be able to do it, every time there's a birth, wedding, engagement, anniversary, anything," Ms. Hugo said.

When Prince William married in 2011, the high-end British department store Fortnum & Mason sold a Wedding Breakfast Blend tea from Kenya, where he proposed. The Lego-themed amusement park Legoland made a brick replica of Buckingham Palace, complete with the bride, groom and assorted well-wishers. The pizza delivery chain Papa John's even turned their faces into a pizza.

Ms. Bridgewater's company has sold over 35,000 pieces of pottery based around Prince William's wedding and has produced 15 different commemorative mugs for events ranging from Prince Andrew and Sarah Ferguson's wedding in 1986, to the birth of Prince William's second child, Princess Charlotte, in 2015. The company has annual sales of about £20 million.

The merchandise this time around is extensive. Ms. Bridgewater has another mug and tea towel planned for the wedding next year, as well as a mug to celebrate the third child of Prince William and Catherine, the Duchess of Cambridge, due in April.

Royal Crown Derby has a series of designs in the works, like a £75 heart-shaped tray and a £150 octagonal plate finished in gold. The company began planning four months before the engagement was officially announced as gossip swirled in the British press.

It is now waiting for specifics, such as whether Ms. Markle will use her given name, Rachel, to put the finishing touches on its fine bone china products. "One of the things that the collectors insist is that it has that level of information and detail applied to the design," said Steven Rowley, Royal Crown Derby's sales and marketing director.

As royal fever grows, the company plans to hire an additional 10 to 15 people. It is also hoping to tap into heightened interest in the United States — Ms. Markle is American — to push its products in places like Bloomingdale's and Bergdorf Goodman.

Tour operators and travel agencies are also gearing up.

British Tours is putting together potential itineraries. The company already runs "Kate and William tours," which follow the footsteps of the royal couple, visiting the town where they went to college and Westminster Abbey, where they married.

Olivia Basic, a tour planner at the company, said the themed tours for Prince Harry and Ms. Markle could include upscale nightclubs where the prince — known in his earlier years for partying heavily — has been spotted.

Others offer a chance to catch a glimpse of the wedding itself. Two days after Prince Harry's engagement was announced, the luxury travel company Noteworthy started scouting locations near the wedding site, St. George's Chapel in Windsor Castle.

Noteworthy is looking to replicate a similar experience during Prince William's wedding. Back then, it hired a place opposite Westminster Abbey so clients — 80 of whom paid £500 each — could watch the bride and groom as they arrived and left the church. For the celebrations commemorating Queen Elizabeth II's Diamond Jubilee, 200 people paid about £300 each to spend the day on the H.M.S. Belfast, a historic warship, to have prime position to watch the monarch's flotilla pageant.

Noteworthy has already secured a location for guests to watch Prince Harry's wedding. But the managing director of Noteworthy, Nicola Butler, declined to say where. She said, however, that it had a view over Windsor Castle's Henry VIII Gate and was "a space that a high-net-worth individual from the U.S. would be comfortable in."

"This," she said, "is really big for us."

Meghan Markle Introduces the British Monarchy to the African-American Experience

BY SARAH LYALL | MAY 19, 2018

LONDON — It was an electrifying and unexpected moment in the midst of what had been a (mostly) by-the-book British wedding service. And as it went on, you could practically feel centuries of tradition begin to peel away.

Here was a relaxed, charismatic African-American bishop — Michael Bruce Curry, the head of the Episcopal Church — speaking to British aristocrats and members of the royal family in the cadence of the black American church.

But what was striking was not just his message, of love and inclusion; or his tone, which was soaring and magisterial; or his obvious delight in the matter at hand. It was the sheer fact of his prominence in a service that featured a fair number of ecclesiastical heavyweights, including the archbishop of Canterbury (who tweeted his admiration of the bishop).

The service, carefully put together by Meghan Markle and Prince Harry, included all the usual traditional elements, like a reading from the Bible by Harry's aunt, the sister of Diana, the Princess of Wales.

It also featured a gorgeous rendition of Ben E. King's "Stand by Me," performed by the Kingdom Choir — a Christian group made up of black Britons that is based in southeast London and specializes in gospel music — and its leader, the renowned gospel singer Karen Gibson.

And it included prayers led by His Eminence Archbishop Angaelos, the Coptic Orthodox archbishop of London; and Rose Hudson-Wilkin, a black Church of England priest who serves as chaplain to the queen and is the speaker's chaplain in the House of Commons.

Bishop Michael Curry cited the words of Martin Luther King Jr. during the wedding ceremony of Prince Harry and Meghan Markle.

And there was a 19-year-old cello soloist, Sheku Kanneh-Mason, the first black musician to win the BBC's Young Musician Award in its 38-year history.

Ms. Markle's mother is African-American and her father is white, and it is clear the bride wanted to make a point of her racial identity, to put her heritage front and center in full view of a vast built-in audience, at home and abroad. And it is equally clear that Prince Harry knew exactly what this would mean to the tradition-bound royal family.

In a place that is so white, in an institution that is so white, in a country with serious race problems, it was a gesture of profound significance. And it was a hugely symbolic moment on a global stage, with the potential to change the world's view of the royal family, and perhaps even Britain's view of itself.

It seems fair to say that never have so many minorities, among the congregation as well as the clergy and musicians, been in St. George's Chapel at one time before.

It was hard to tell, looking out over the church crowd, what the general reaction was to Bishop Curry's address. Some people looked a little bemused; a couple of royals looked as if they were on the verge of giggling, at least according to the The Daily Mail, which likes to stir up trouble, in this case with mild insinuation.

The bishop himself seemed to sense he was speaking longer than perhaps some in the crowd were accustomed to, although he was not particularly fussed about it. At one point, he appeared to hurry himself along, telling the couple teasingly: "We gotta get y'all married." (Not everyone knew how to cope with that American expression; the BBC rendered it "you all" in its transcript.)

But outside the ancient walls of the chapel and across the country, the response was jubilant. It was as if Bishop Curry had opened the windows and let a breath of air into a room that had felt a little stifling.

People in Britain do not usually speak of love in the way he did in church. People here do not usually express themselves so forthrightly.

"The preacher is doing 50 in a 30 zone and it's brilliant," the BBC presenter Jeremy Vine wrote on Twitter.

Also on Twitter, a woman named Andrea L. Pinto wrote: "Rev. Michael Curry is talking about slaves finding love in the South in the face of the Queen of England. This moment is hundreds of years in the making."

In another Twitter post, from North Carolina, Chris Burris said: "Bishop Michael Curry is quoting Dr. Martin Luther King Jr. at Windsor Castle. It's truly a day of wonders."

It was indeed an amazing thing to hear Dr. King's words spoken on an occasion like this. They felt appropriate to the moment — this was, after all, a wedding — but had a larger significance, about the world in general and how we should conduct ourselves.

"We must discover the power of love, the redemptive power of love," Bishop Curry said, quoting Dr. King. "And when we do that, we will make of this old world, a new world."

Glossary

abdicate To give up one's throne or reject a responsibility.

Anglican Relating to the institution, theological concepts, or liturgical traditions developed by the Church of England.

aristocracy A hereditary high class rank or form of government by such indviduals.

Austerity Britain A condition under which the United Kingdom reduces public spending to stabilize the economy.

bank holiday A public holiday in the United Kingdom.

blackamoor Blackamoor figurines or jewelery are a style of small figures that depict men or women with black skin. 'Blackamoor' is an outdated term for a person with dark skin. Both the term and the figurines are seen as offensive.

Brexit An abbreviation for 'British exit,' referring to the country's decision to exit the European Union.

Buckingham Palace Built in 1703, Buckingham Palace has been the official London residence and administrative headquarters of the British monarch since 1837.

Church of England The established state church in England and mother church of the Anglican Communion. The monarch is the supreme governer of the church.

commoner A person without a title of nobility.

courtship A period of time in which a couple develops a romantic relationship, often with the goal of marriage.

duke and duchess In European nobility, a duke (male) or duchess (female) is the highest rank below the monarch. A duke or duchess owns a portion of land or real estate.

heir A person who has the right to inherit a title or property after the death of its owner.

House of Windsor The royal house of Britain, renamed in 1917.

Labour Party A political party in the U.K. that generally advocates for democratic socialism.

monarchy A form of government in which a single person reigns.

parliament A legislative body of government that, in Britain, consists of the monarch, the House of Commons, and the House of Lords.

posh Elegant, fashionable or upper class.

primogeniture A right of inheritance belonging to a firstborn child.

prince or princess The son (prince) or daughter (princess) of a monarch. The wife of a prince may also be called a princess.

referendum A direct vote on one political question.

Republican Party In Britain, a political movement that seeks to replace the monarchy with a republic.

sovereign A king, queen or person having the supreme power to govern a country.

St. James Palace One of London's oldest palaces and significant ceremonial meeting places.

succession The process and order in which one person inherits a title or land from another.

Trafalgar Square The largest public square in the city of Westminster, Central London.

Westminster Abbey The site of coronations and other events of national importance.

Windsor Castle The oldest and largest English royal residence.

Media Literacy Terms

"Media literacy" refers to the ability to access, understand, critically assess and create media. The following terms are important components of media literacy, and they will help you critically engage with the articles in this title.

angle The aspect of a news story that a journalist focuses on and develops.

attribution The method by which a source is identified or by which facts and information are assigned to the person who provided them.

balance Principle of journalism that both perspectives of an argument should be presented in a fair way.

bias A disposition of prejudice in favor of a certain idea, person, or perspective.

byline Name of the writer, usually placed between the headline and the story.

caption Identifying copy for a picture; also called a legend or cutline.

chronological order Method of writing a story presenting the details of the story in the order in which they occurred.

column Type of story that is a regular feature, often on a recurring topic, written by the same journalist, generally known as a columnist.

commentary Type of story that is an expression of opinion on recent events by a journalist generally known as a commentator.

credibility The quality of being trustworthy and believable, said of a journalistic source.

editorial Article of opinion or interpretation.

feature story Article designed to entertain as well as to inform.

headline Type, usually 18 point or larger, used to introduce a story.

human interest story Type of story that focuses on individuals and how events or issues affect their lives, generally offering a sense of relatability to the reader.

impartiality Principle of journalism that a story should not reflect a journalist's bias and should contain balance.

intention The motive or reason behind something, such as the publication of a news story.

interview story Type of story in which the facts are gathered primarily by interviewing another person or persons.

motive The reason behind something, such as the publication of a news story or a source's perspective on an issue.

news story An article or style of expository writing that reports news, generally in a straightforward fashion and without editorial comment.

op-ed An opinion piece that reflects a prominent journalist's opinion on a topic of interest.

paraphrase The summary of an individual's words, with attribution, rather than a direct quotation of their exact words.

plagiarism An attempt to pass another person's work as one's own without attribution.

quotation The use of an individual's exact words indicated by the use of quotation marks and proper attribution.

reliability The quality of being dependable and accurate, said of a journalistic source.

source The origin of the information reported in journalism.

tone A manner of expression in writing or speech.

Media Literacy Questions

1. In "An Ocean of Union Jacks and Chanting Throngs Along Procession Route" (on page 32), William Borders directly quotes procession spectators. What are the strengths of using direct quotations as opposed to paraphrasing? What are the weaknesses?

2. Compare the headlines of "Charles and Diana Are Separating 'Amicably' " (on page 40) and "Whispers, Anger and Doubt As Britons Rally to Princess" (on page 36). Which is a more compelling headline, and why? How could the less compelling headline be changed to draw better the reader's interest?

3. "Passion Versus Pageantry in Royal Wedding Reports" (on page 95) features a photograph. What does this photograph add to the article?

4. What type of story is "Prince William and Kate Try to Seem Normal" (on page 107)? Can you identify another article in this collection that is the same type of story?

5. What angle did the journalist take in the article "Royal Engagement Seen as Symbol of Change, With Asterisks" (on page 161)? What is gained by taking that angle?

6. Does Kimiko de Freytas-Tamura demonstrate the journalistic principle of balance and impartiality in her article "Prince Harry, Meghan Markle, and News of a Royal Wedding" (on page 127)? If so, how did she do so? If not, what could she have included to make her article more balanced and impartial?

Citations

All citations in this list are formatted according to the Modern Language Association's (MLA) style guide.

BOOK CITATION

NEW YORK TIMES EDITORIAL STAFF, THE. *Royal Couples: Harry and Meghan Markle, William and Kate Middleton, and Charles and Diana.* New York: New York Times Educational Publishing, 2019.

ARTICLE CITATIONS

APPLE JR., R.W. "Americans and Royalty: Symbols Clash No More." *The New York Times*, 5 Nov. 1985, https://www.nytimes.com/1985/11/05/us/americans -and-royalty-symbols-clash-no-more.html.

APPLE JR., R.W. "Charles and Lady Diana Rehearse the Wedding." *The New York Times*, 28 Jul. 1981, https://www.nytimes.com/1981/07/28/world/ charles-and-lady-diana-rehearse-the-wedding.html.

BARRY, ELLEN. "As Prince Harry and Meghan Markle Wed, a New Era Dawns." *The New York Times*, 19 May 2018, https://www.nytimes.com/2018/05/19/ world/europe/meghan-markle-prince-harry-wedding.html.

BENNHOLD, KATRIN. "A Royal Christening in Britain Amid a Refrain of Coos." *The New York Times*, 23 Oct. 2013, http://www.nytimes.com/2013/10/24/ world/europe/royal-christening-draws-patient-crowds-in-london.html.

BLUMENTHAL, RALPH. "Prince Harry, in His Mother's Footsteps." *The New York Times*, 29 May 2009, http://www.nytimes.com/2009/05/30/nyregion/ 30prince.html.

BORDERS, WILLIAM. "An Ocean of Union Jacks and Chanting Throngs Along Procession Route." *The New York Times*, 30 Jul. 1981, https://www.nytimes. com/1981/07/30/world/an-ocean-of-union-jacks-and-chanting-throngs -along-procession-route.html.

BORDERS, WILLIAM. "Royal Romance and Princely Duty." *The New York Times*,

22 Mar. 1981, https://www.nytimes.com/1981/03/22/magazine/royal
-romance-and-princely-duty.html

BROWN, ROBBIE. "Gearing Up for Distant Royal 'I Dos.'" *The New York Times*,
18 Nov. 2010, http://www.nytimes.com/2010/11/19/us/19marietta.html.

BURNS, JOHN F. "British Monarchy Scraps Rule of Male Succession in New
Step to Modernization." *The New York Times*, 28 Oct. 2011, http://www
.nytimes.com/2011/10/29/world/europe/rule-of-male-succession-to-british
-monarchy-is-abolished.html.

BURNS, JOHN F. "For Prince Harry, Vegas Exploits Didn't Stay There." *The
New York Times*, 23 Aug. 2012, https://archive.nytimes.com/query.nytimes
.com/gst/fullpage-9E06EFD9133AF930A1575BC0A9649D8B63.html.

BURNS, JOHN F. "In This Fairy Tale, Not One, but Two Queens in Waiting."
The New York Times, 18 Apr. 2011, https://www.nytimes.com/2011/04/19/
world/europe/19wedding.html.

CHOKSHI, NIRAJ. "Prince Harry Used Princess Diana's Diamonds in Engagement Ring." *The New York Times*, 27 Nov. 2017, https://www.nytimes.com/
2017/11/27/world/europe/prince-harry-engagement-ring.html.

DRAKE, MONICA. "A Mixed-Race Royal Couple? It Wouldn't Be the First." *The
New York Times*, 30 Nov. 2017, https://www.nytimes.com/2017/11/30/us/
black-princess-meghan-markle.html.

ERLANGER, STEVEN. "Kate, Duchess of Cambridge, Gives Birth to Baby Girl."
The New York Times, 2 May 2015, https://www.nytimes.com/2015/05/03/
world/europe/former-kate-middleton-duchess-of-cambridge-gives-birth-to
-baby-girl.html.

ERLANGER, STEVEN. "Prince Harry Denounces Media Coverage of His Girlfriend, Meghan Markle." *The New York Times*, 8 Nov. 2016, https://www
.nytimes.com/2016/11/09/world/europe/prince-harry-girlfriend-meghan
-markle.html.

DE FREYTAS-TAMURA, KIMIKO. "Prince Harry, Meghan Markle and News of a
Royal Wedding." *The New York Times*, 27 Nov. 2017, https://www.nytimes.
com/2017/11/27/world/europe/prince-harry-meghan-markle-engaged.html.

DE FREYTAS-TAMURA, KIMIKO. "So, Meghan Markle, Are You Familiar With the
Statute of Rhuddlan?" *The New York Times*, 2 Dec. 2017, https://www
.nytimes.com/2017/12/02/world/europe/uk-citizenship-meghan-markle.html.

FRIEDMAN, VANESSA. "Meghan Markle Is Going to Make History." *The New
York Times*, 27 Nov. 2017, https://www.nytimes.com/2017/11/27/fashion/
meghan-markle-prince-harry-wedding-style.html.

FRIEDMAN, VANESSA. "Meghan Markle's Sheer Top Was a Sneaky Statement for a Royal Portrait." *The New York Times*, 22 Dec. 2017, https://www .nytimes.com/2017/12/22/fashion/meghan-markle-engagement-portrait -dress.html.

FRIEDMAN, VANESSA. "Prince William and Kate Try to Seem Normal." *The New York Times*, 10 Dec. 2014, https://www.nytimes.com/2014/12/11/fashion/ prince-william-and-kate-try-to-seem-normal.html.

HAUGHNEY, CHRISTINE. "Celebrity Weeklies Are Reveling in a Royal Baby, and Sales." *The New York Times*, 11 Aug. 2013, http://www.nytimes.com/2013/ 08/12/business/media/celebrity-weeklies-are-reveling-in-a-royal-baby-and -sales.html.

HAUSER, CHRISTINE. "British Royal Weddings and the Barriers That Fell With Them." *The New York Times*, 27 Nov. 2011, https://www.nytimes .com/2017/11/27/world/europe/british-royal-weddings.html.

HAUSER, CHRISTINE. "Who Wants to Be King? No One, Prince Harry Says." *The New York Times*, 22 Jun. 2017, https://www.nytimes.com/2017/06/22/ world/europe/prince-harry-monarchy-britain.html.

KINGSLEY, PATRICK. "Royal Engagement Seen as Symbol of Change, With Asterisks." *The New York Times*, 28 Nov. 2017, https://www.nytimes.com/ 2017/11/28/world/europe/uk-royal-wedding-harry-meghan-markle.html.

LYALL, SARAH. "A Traditional Royal Wedding, but for the 3 Billion Witnesses." *The New York Times*, 29 Apr. 2011, http://www.nytimes.com/2011/04/30/ world/europe/30britain.html.

LYALL, SARAH. "British Royal Wedding Set for April 29." *The New York Times*, 23 Nov. 2010, http://www.nytimes.com/2010/11/24/world/europe/24royal.html.

LYALL, SARAH. "Britons Strike Sour Notes on Royal Wedding." *The New York Times*, 18 Feb. 2005, http://www.nytimes.com/2005/02/18/world/europe/ britons-strike-sour-noteson-royal-wedding.html.

LYALL, SARAH. "Charles and Camilla, Married at Last, and With Hardly a Hitch." *The New York Times*, 10 Apr. 2005, http://www.nytimes.com/2005/04/10/world/ europe/charles-and-camilla-married-at-last-and-with-hardly-a-hitch.html.

LYALL, SARAH. "Charles and Diana Agree on Divorce Terms." *The New York Times*, 13 Jul. 1996, http://www.nytimes.com/1996/07/13/world/charles -and-diana-agree-on-divorce-terms.html.

LYALL, SARAH. "Diana's Legacy: A Reshaped Monarchy, a More Emotional U.K." *The New York Times*, 30 Aug. 2017, https://www.nytimes.com/2017/ 08/30/world/europe/princess-diana-death-anniversary.html.

LYALL, SARAH. "Diana's Ring Seals Prince William's Marriage Plans." *The New York Times*, 16 Nov. 2010, http://www.nytimes.com/2010/11/17/world/europe/17royal.html.

LYALL, SARAH. "Fixating on a Future Royal as Elusive as Cinderella." *The New York Times*, 21 Apr. 2011, http://www.nytimes.com/2011/04/21/world/europe/21kate.html.

LYALL, SARAH. "For Charles, Camilla and Britain, the Wait Is Over." *The New York Times*, 9 Apr. 2005, http://www.nytimes.com/2005/04/09/world/europe/for-charles-camilla-and-britain-the-wait-is-over.html.

LYALL, SARAH. "For Media and the Royals, Earl Takes Off His Gloves." *The New York Times*, 7 Sep. 1997, http://www.nytimes.com/1997/09/07/world/for-media-and-the-royals-earl-takes-off-his-gloves.html.

LYALL, SARAH. "It's Official: Charles and Diana Split, and She Pays Her Own Bills." *The New York Times*, 29 Aug. 1996, http://www.nytimes.com/1996/08/29/world/it-s-official-charles-and-diana-split-and-she-pays-her-own-bills.html.

LYALL, SARAH. "Major Royal News. Impose Story of Your Choice." *The New York Times*, 19 May. 2018, https://www.nytimes.com/2018/05/19/world/europe/uk-royal-black-priest-choir.html.

LYALL, SARAH. "Meghan Markle Introduces the British Monarchy to the African-American Experience." *The New York Times*, 3 Dec. 2017, https://www.nytimes.com/2017/12/03/insider/major-royal-news-impose-story-of-your-choice.html.

LYALL, SARAH. "Prince Harry Casts Aside Ghosts of Royal Marriages Past." *The New York Times*, 11 Nov. 2017, https://www.nytimes.com/2017/11/27/world/europe/prince-harry-meghan-markle-engagement-royal.html.

MENKES, SUZY. "Royals Show Little Affinity for Rank as They Take Spouses." *The New York Times*, 16 Nov. 2010, http://www.nytimes.com/2010/11/17/world/europe/17iht-wedding.html.

THE NEW YORK TIMES. "The Prince and the Actress." *The New York Times*, 29 Nov. 2017, https://www.nytimes.com/2017/11/29/opinion/prince-harry-meghan-markle.html.

OKOJIE, IRENOSEN. "Can Meghan Markle Save the Monarchy?" *The New York Times*, 28 Nov. 2017, https://www.nytimes.com/2017/11/28/opinion/prince-harry-meghan-markle-monarchy.html.

RATTNER, STEVEN. "For an English Town, Wedding Madness and History." *The New York Times*, 24 Jul. 1981, https://www.nytimes.com/1981/07/24/world/

for-an-english-town-wedding-madness-and-history.html.

SCHMIDT, WILLIAM E. "Charles and Diana Are Separating 'Amicably.' " *The New York Times*, 10 Dec. 1992, https://www.nytimes.com/1992/12/10/world/charles-and-diana-are-separating-amicably.html.

SCHMIDT, WILLIAM E. "Whispers, Anger and Doubt As Britons Rally to Princess." *The New York Times*, 20 Jun. 1992, https://www.nytimes.com/1992/06/20/world/whispers-anger-and-doubt-as-britons-rally-to-princess.html.

SOMAIYA, RAVI. "In Media's Wedding Frenzy, Hints of Viewer Fatigue." *The New York Times*, 22 Apr. 2011, http://www.nytimes.com/2011/04/23/world/europe/23wedding.html.

STACK, LIAM. "Do Americans Love the British Royal Family? Quite." *The New York Times*, 4 Dec. 2017, https://www.nytimes.com/2017/12/04/style/british-royal-americans.html.

STANLEY, ALESSANDRA. "Passion Versus Pageantry in Royal Wedding Reports." *The New York Times*, 29 Apr. 2011, http://www.nytimes.com/2011/04/30/arts/television/in-royal-wedding-television-coverage-british-and-americans-differ-tv-watch.html

STANLEY, ALESSANDRA. "Toasts for Royals, Spiked With Scorn." *The New York Times*, 20 Apr. 2011, http://www.nytimes.com/2011/04/24/arts/television/toasts-to-prince-william-and-kate-middleton-spiked-with-scorn.html.

TREBAY, GUY. "Prince Harry, Almost Just Like Us." *The New York Times*, 17 May 2013, http://www.nytimes.com/2013/05/19/fashion/prince-harry-draws-a-crowd-at-the-greenwich-polo-club.html.

TSANG, AMIE. "Prince Harry Is Getting Married. Time for Themed Mugs and Nightclub Tours." *The New York Times*, 24 Dec. 2017, https://www.nytimes.com/2017/12/24/business/prince-harry-meghan-markle-wedding.html.

WERDIGIER, JULIA. "Books, Brioche and Baby Clothes: The Royal Merchandise." *The New York Times*, 22 Jul. 2013, https://thelede.blogs.nytimes.com/2013/07/22/books-brioche-and-baby-clothes-the-royal-merchandise.

YEGINSU, CEYLAN. "Prince Harry and Meghan Markle Invite Members of Public to Wedding Day." *The New York Times*, 2 Mar. 18, https://www.nytimes.com/2018/03/02/world/europe/uk-prince-harry-meghan-markle-wedding.html.

Index